The Enneagram
and Kabbalah

The Enneagram and Kabbalah

Reading Your Soul

Rabbi Howard A. Addison

For People of All Faiths, All Backgrounds
JEWISH LIGHTS PUBLISHING
Woodstock, Vermont

The Enneagram and Kabbalah: Reading Your Soul

Library of Congress Cataloging-in-Publication Data
Addison, Howard A., 1950–
    The enneagram and kabbalah : reading your soul / by
Howard A. Addison
        p.   cm.
    Includes bibliographical references.
    ISBN 1-58023-001-6 (pb)
    1. Spiritual life—Judaism. 2. Self-perception—
Religious aspects—Judaism. 3. Self-actualization
(Psychology)—Religious aspects—Judaism.
4. Enneagram. 5. Sefirot (Cabala) I. Title.
BM723.A33   1998
296.7—dc21   98–10641
                                                  CIP

First Edition

10 9 8 7 6 5 4 3 2 1

Manufactured in the United States of America
Jacket design by Bronwen Battaglia
Text design by Sans Serif Inc.

For People of All Faiths, All Backgrounds

Published by Jewish Lights Publishing
A Division of LongHill Partners Inc.
Sunset Farm Offices, Route 4
P.O. Box 237
Woodstock, Vermont 05091
Tel: (802) 457-4000   Fax: (802) 457-4004
www.jewishlights.com

Contents

Prologue

As a younger man, I was thrilled by the tales of Kabbalists and Hasidic masters. I marveled at the spiritual power of their teachings and the magnetism of their personalities. Most fascinating of all were their powers of clairvoyance. Again and again, I would wonder at the abilities of people like Rabbi Yaakov Yizhak Halevi Horowitz, the nineteenth-century Seer of Lublin who could read people's souls. Supposedly he could tell by glancing at someone's forehead from which location on the Tree of Life their spirit had descended and what their destiny would be.

Years elapsed since I first pondered that aspect of Jewish mysticism, and other considerations drew my attention. Yet in February 1995 my interest in mysticism was reignited. The occasion was a Spirituality seminar sponsored by the Alban Institute, an interdenominational center near Washington, D.C., that offers continuing training for clergy and congregational leaders. There, through the tutelage of Roy Oswald, I was introduced to the Enneagram.

Two aspects of the Enneagram affected me profoundly at the seminar. The first was the Enneagram's powerful insights. In the past other methods of personality typing such as Myers-Briggs had helped me understand my own character and how it interacted with the styles of others. Learning my Enneagram number proved nothing short of transformative. To find my weakness revealed as the shadow side of my strength, to discover that what I had considered my noble accomplishments were motivated, in part, by ignoble intent was profound and changed my spiritual outlook.

The relationship between the Enneagram and

Kabbalah (Jewish mysticism) also struck me during the seminar. While the two systems are not identical, their points of correspondence seemed almost self-evident. Drawing on similar ancient and medieval sources, the nine points on the Enneagram and the ten *sefirot* (potencies) on the Tree of Life, the *Etz Chayim* each posit a correlation between the structure of reality and the soul. My subsequent reading in the history and insights of the Enneagram and Kabbalistic psychology have given ongoing confirmation to my initial impressions of a correspondence between the two systems.

At the end of the seminar, I asked Roy Oswald to recommend the best single book on the Enneagram. Without hesitation, he mentioned *The Enneagram* by Helen Palmer. I immediately purchased the book and read it cover to cover several times. In turn, I enrolled in her training seminars. Helen's teaching of the Enneagram, its personality subtypes, the levels of human consciousness and how we filter information and place our attention are deeply original. While the correlations to the Kabbalah found in this text are mine, they rely upon the pioneering work of Helen Palmer and her insightful co-teacher, Dr. David Daniels.

I wrote this book for several reasons. Academically, I am interested in the parallel development of the Enneagram and Kabbalah and their points of correspondence. My own analysis indicates that the two systems of personality should be correlated differently than they have been in the past. While allusions and references to the Kabbalah/Enneagram connection can be found in previous Enneagram literature, there is a need for greater exploration and detail. I hope that this work provides some initial steps in that direction.

Also, I believe that knowledge of the Enneagram can provide those familiar with the Kabbalah (and those who would like to be) with a powerful tool for self-knowledge, critique and transformation. Jewish tradition maintains that a sacred text can be read on four levels: *Peshat,* its historical, exoteric meaning; *Remez,* the literary and verbal allusions which link it to other passages and contexts; *D'rash,* its sermonic lessons; and *Sod,* its hidden sense which mystically points the way to ultimate meaning. In that text known as the human heart, the Enneagram functions on the deepest level, that of *Sod.*

People who are moved to religious inquiry want to know where to begin. Common wisdom usually counsels the reading of some introductory literature and trying some of the major spiritual practices of the faith that is under consideration. Perhaps a more personalized road would also include discovering our own personality type with its strengths and weaknesses. Such a discovery could be essential to finding our own spiritual gateway to God within the tradition we are exploring.

This book is not meant to be an extensive introduction to Kabbalah or an authoritative study of the Enneagram. Instead, its first section provides an overview of both systems and insights on points of correspondence between the two. The second section examines through the lens of Kabbalah the dynamics and characteristics of the nine personality types and suggests some introductory Jewish observances that should appeal to each. It will then offer some advanced spiritual tasks appropriate for the growth of each type as prescribed by the sixteenth-century mystic, Rabbi Moshe Cordevero. These religious practices were set forth as ways in which the seeker could identify with the qualities of each *sefirah.* My own interpretation of his prescriptions led me to the conclusion that the tasks for each *sefirah* are indeed appropriate for its corresponding Enneagram personality type.

It is my prayer that the insights which follow combined with the specified practices of worship, study and loving deeds will help open the gateway to self-awareness while pointing us personally toward our own heaven's door.

Acknowledgments

All materials in this text which describe the shift from higher to lower consciousness, from the realm of Essence to Personality with its manifestations as subtype behavior, and the path from vice to virtue conversion, are derived from the ground-breaking Enneagram work of Helen Palmer and Dr. David Daniels.

For that, I honor and thank them.

Two Diagrams
of Life

1

"Where Are You?"

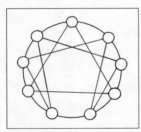 EXAMINE THE FIRST CHAPTER OF Genesis and you will discover an amazing truth. In six days, God separated light from darkness, heaven from earth, dry land from the seas. Plant life and all kinds of swimming, flying and prowling creatures were called into being. However, only as the sixth day waned did God preface action with an announcement: Adam would be created in God's image and likeness. Only then did God form humans, male and female, in God's divine image.

This tale suggests that, even before we humans come into being, God knows us and calls us by name. Yet as our lives unfold, we forget our true selves and turn an increasingly deaf ear to that divine call. We grow from infancy to childhood to adolescence to adulthood developing strategies to navigate the pathways of life. We do this with greater or less success. These responses and habits become the features of our acquired personality, the face we present to the world—and even to ourselves—as we react to life's situations.

As time passes, however, we may begin feeling uneasy with our accustomed roles, with the near-scripted ways that we react to others.

Why do I always pick a fight, even before someone else has said or done anything offensive?

Is there a reason why everyone brings their troubles to me? I'm always meeting their needs, and yet I can never recognize my needs.

A sense of dissonance can develop between our acquired personalities and the "real me" which feels trapped inside and yearns to be free. We might try to take action and not know where to begin. Having become accustomed to our acquired way of being, we are unable to risk acting differently lest we lose the comfort of what we know so well. In Genesis, God called to Adam with the word "*Ayeka,*" "Where are you?" Don't we, like Adam, hide from that divine call, covering our true self with the fig leaf of our rationalizations and habituated responses?

Actually, our acquired personalities are not bad things at all. Born of our own innate temperament and our perceptions and experiences, they provide us with the means to relate to other people and our environment. They cushion our essential selves from the hurt that comes from living in the world. While acting as shields and buffers, these acquired personalities can also be the starting points on our path to truth—if we recognize them. As Psalm 29 proclaims, "The voice of the Lord comes in strength." The sages of Israel interpreted this to mean that God's voice does not summon us uniformly, according to God's own strength. Instead, God calls to us individually according to our own strengths and character. Legend maintains that God's revelation at Mount Sinai was conveyed through 600,000 different channels, one for each person present. Therefore, if we seek God's personal message that is meant only for us, we might begin by learning about ourselves and our own traits.

Parallel Maps of Our Inner Universe

How can we distinguish between these acquired personality traits and the essential self hidden underneath? According to the Kabbalah, the source of each soul is rooted in a different aspect of the divine personality. The configuration of that divine personality and its ten characteristics (*sefirot*) is alternately known as *Adam Kadmon,* the Primordial Man, or *Etz Chayim,* the Tree of Life. The search for the essential self beneath the shroud of personality might well lie in tracing back the root of each soul to its point of origin. To aid us in this quest we might call upon the Enneagram.

The Enneagram is a nine-pointed star. The origins of the diagram itself are somewhat shrouded in mystery. Some attribute its beginning to a sect of medieval Islamic mystics still in existence today known as the Sufis. Others trace its origins to the work of ancient Greek philosophers or even farther back to a Mesopotamian wisdom school in the late third millennium B.C.E. called the Sarmoun Brotherhood.[1]

Like the Tree of Life, the Enneagram is considered to depict not only the structure of ultimate reality, but also different core aspects of personality. The nine points along the Enneagram represent nine different human personality types. Each of us predominantly manifests the traits of our own particular type under normal conditions. The Enneagram is enclosed by a circle which connects the nine points around its circumference, indicating that each type might share some traits with either (or both) "Wing" points on its two sides. The points of the diagram are connected internally by lines whose distinct pattern indicates how our basic personality moves toward adopting some characteristics of another specific type when we experience undue stress and toward adopting some traits of a third type when we are feeling comfortable and secure.

As we shall see in the chapters to come, the *Etz Chayim* and the Enneagram draw upon many common historical sources and share several points of correspondence. Perhaps their most profound joint assertion is that our highest virtues and most troubling vices are actually rooted in the same source. Kabbalists have described the domain of evil as the *Sitra Achra,* literally the "Other Side" of the Tree of Life. The Enneagram teaching demonstrates how the giving person can use generosity to manipulate others or how perfectionists use the pursuit of correctness as testimony to their own superiority.

According to Jewish tradition, God fashioned human beings not with one inclination, but with two: the *Yetser HaTov,* our selfless inclination, and the *Yetser HaRa,* our self-serving, even harmful inclination.[2] Therefore, only by recognizing and confronting both sides of our creation can we begin the path toward redemption.

In Exodus, we learn that Moses climbed again to the top of Mount Sinai following the Sin of the Golden Calf and the shattering of the Ten Commandments tablets. There, Moses' skin hardened as his face began radiating power and light.[3] Afterwards, he always wore a veil while interacting with others. Only before God did Moses remove his veil, and his naked face appeared in all its toughness and its brilliance.

To get along in this world each of us, of necessity, acquires a veil of personality. This lets us interact with our world while protecting the privacy of the inner self. It can, however, become suffocating at some juncture in life. If we pull back our veils and reveal our features in all their coarseness and all their brilliance, then maybe we, like Moses, can use that revealing as the starting point for our discourse with God.

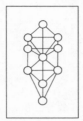

2

The Tree Of Life

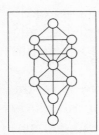 THE FIRST WORD FOUND IN THE TORAH is *"Bereshit—*In the beginning." The first Hebrew letter of this first word is *"Bet."* Since each Hebrew letter has a numerical value, we might have expected the first letter of scripture to be *"Aleph,"* the first character in the Hebrew alphabet and the letter which equals one. Why begin the Torah with *"Bet,"* which stands for the number two? While many explanations have been offered for this apparent anomaly, a Kabbalistic interpretation alludes to creation as a dual rather than a singular process. The Creation story in Genesis is seen mystically as the outer manifestation of a more sublime unfolding. Just as our physical world was being fashioned, so the unknowable, boundless God, *Ayn Sof,* was also calling into being the configuration of God's own divine personality. This configuration, the *Etz Chayim* or Tree of Life, is composed

of ten different characteristics. It is both the substructure, the hidden reality, of all that exists as well as the way in which God's creatures can recognize and come to know their creator.

Attempts to describe *Echad,* the One God, as subsuming ten powers actually predates Kabbalah. Early rabbinic sources not only speak of the Divine One who created the world through Ten Creative Utterances,[4] but also connect these ten utterances to the Ten Plagues and the Ten Commandments.[5] These Ten Utterances, however, are considered to be more than God's creative expressions. Their role as divine agencies instrumental in fashioning the cosmos is made explicit in a later Talmudic text.[6]

Because of its mysterious nature, many different explanations can be found in Kabbalistic literature describing the relationship between the *Ayn Sof,* the boundless, unknowable God, and the ten characteristics of the divine personality, the *sefirot.* Some see the *sefirot* as merely ten different external features of the *Ayn Sof* itself, like a jewel and its facets. Others view them as ten instruments of divine power or as ten receptacles of *Shefa,* the divine radiant energy which emanates from *Ayn Sof* toward our world.

The *sefirot* are also known as God's Crowns or the names God calls Godself. The configuration of the *sefirot* has been depicted in a variety of tree, human and geometric shapes. Mystical thinkers even differ over the numbering of the *sefirot.*

The following is a short synopsis of the *sefirot* and a common diagram of the *Etz Chayim:*

Keter   Supernal Crown, the point of transition from potential to actuality, from *Ayn Sof* to the *Etz Chayim.* It can be compared to the initial point where pen touches paper before writing begins, like the jot on top of the *Yod* (ׁ) the first

Hebrew letter of the Tetragramaton (YHWH), the four-letter name of God.

Chochmah	Wisdom, also known as Supernal Father, *Abba*. Encapsulated within it are the encoded archetypes of all being.
Binah	Understanding, also called *Ima*, Supernal Mother. Being differentiates and unfolds within *Binah* the way the zygote develops into the various organs and limbs of the fetus in the womb.
Gedulah	Greatness or *Chesed*, "Kindness," which is the creative force of God's love.
Din	Judgment or *Gevurah*, "Power." This is the aspect of God that sets limits and boundaries. *Din* is to *Chesed* as form is to content.
Tiferet	Beauty that comes when *Chesed* and *Din* are in balance.
Netsach	The eternal, enduring nature of God.
Hod	Divine splendor.
Yesod	Foundation, alternately called *Tsadik*, "Righteous," for the "righteous are the foundation of the world" (Proverbs 10:25). When the ten *sefirot* are depicted in human form, *Yesod* corresponds to the male generative organ, since it focuses the *Shefa's* potency from the upper *sefirot* and emits it downward.
Shechinah	God's Indwelling Presence or Nearness. Like *Binah*, it is a feminine aspect of God, and receives the *Shefa* from *Yesod* and *Tiferet* above. Pictured as bride or sister, *Shechinah* is the

DIAGRAM 1

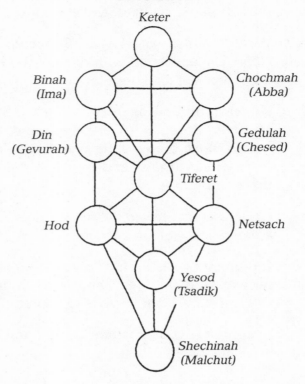

sefirah closest to our physical world. It is also known as *Malchut*—God's sovereignty.

The relationship among the *sefirot* is anything but static, and their connection to our world is hardly simple. The divine radiance of *Shefa* races back and forth among the various *sefirot,* whose balance is quite precarious. This process, known as *Ratso Va Shov,* "Egress and Return," proceeds in a lightening bolt, zigzag fashion along twenty-two paths (see Diagram 1) that correspond to the number of letters in the Hebrew *Aleph-Bet. Sefer Yetsirah,* an early Jewish mystical work, considered the number ten, which corresponds to the prime numbers in the decimal system, and the twenty-two letters of Hebrew, the language of God's Ten Creative Utterances, to have played an instrumental role in God's creation of the world.

Ancient physics maintained that the four essential elements of our world—Fire, Air, Water and Earth—form a chain of ever-increasing physical density. So the Kabbalistic schema posits the descent of our physical world from the divinity of *Ayn Sof* as gravitating down through four worlds of increasing coarseness. Each of these four worlds (*Olam Ha'atsilut,* the World of Divine Emanation; *Olam Ha Beriah,* the World of Creating; *Olam Ha Yetsirah,* the World of Formation; and *Olam Ha-asiyah,* the archetype of our World of Physical Action) is undergirded by its own representation of the *Etz Chayim.* The worlds are connected by the final *sefirah, Shechinah,* of the preceding world's Tree of Life, which also serves as the first *sefirah, Keter,* of the next world's *Etz Chayim.*

Kabbalistic Psychology

Rabbinic lore claims that before the Fall, Adam was an ethereal human-shaped creature who was so immense that he straddled the earth from one end to the other. This vast cosmic being was known as *Adam Kadmon,* Primordial Man. But with the Fall, this spiritlike individual lost its aura, became a physical creature and was reduced to human proportions. This downsized mortal was then called *Adam Rishon,* the First Man of the later Genesis tales.

Given the Torah's depiction of God's features and emotions in personal terms and given its claim that people were created in God's image, it is hardly surprising that Jewish mystics depicted the divine in terms of the human figure. *Shiur Komah,* a second- to sixth-century C.E. mystical movement, produced literature describing God's appearance. Reading Song of Songs as an allegory of God's love for Israel, *Shiur Komah* described God's features as

DIAGRAM 2

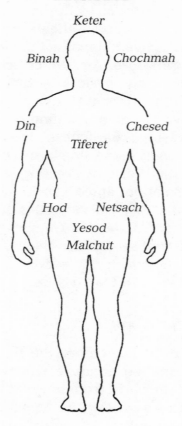

being identical to those of the Song's lover, only of mammoth size. Later Kabbalists adapted the figure of *Adam Kadmon,* the cosmic-sized Adam, as an alternative to the *Etz Chayim* for depicting the configuration of the ten *sefirot.* Since Genesis tells us that God created Adam as both male and female, the *Adam Kadmon* of the *sefirot* is male and female joined in coitus.

Just as the *sefirot* form the substructure of the cosmos, they also underlie what we are as human beings. As the worldly embodiments of Adam, our psyches contain all the potentialities of *Adam Kadmon*. The interaction of the various *sefirot* engender different aspects of our psyche's function. Our creature vitality, *Nefesh,* which we share in common with the animal world, emanates from the last *sefirah, Shechinah* or *Malchut*. Since its seat is in the lower abdominal region, perhaps this is why we refer to our unconscious survival instincts as "gut feelings."

When this *sefirah* interacts with the heart-centered *Tiferet,* the social and emotional inner self of *Ruah* arises, which lifts us beyond our purely vitalistic side. *Neshamah,* which is born of the head-centered *Binah,* is both our speculative reason and the intuitive power of mind and soul which directly connects us to God. Interestingly, *Neshamah* literally translates as "breath," and it is through meditative breath exercise and prayer that we can summon our higher observing mind. Detached from worldly distractions, it enables us to sense that our essential self is different from our perceptions and automatic emotional responses. It is at this level of *Neshamah* that our souls have the possibility of bonding with the divine.[7]

If we each share *Adam Kadmon*'s potencies, how do we derive our individuality? Three different phenomena account for this. In a Kabbalistic reading of the "Fall," Adam's sin lied in detaching *Malchut,* God's earthly presence and the lowest *sefirah,* from the rest of the Tree of Life. The reason was that Adam mistakenly considered *Malchut* to be the whole of divinity. Through this act of Adam, our lower will parted from the divine, the uninterrupted communion of the *sefirot* with one another was severed and a multiplicity of worlds and creatures and souls proliferated.

While each of us has all the *sefirotic* potentialities, the root of our individual souls comes from the individual *sefirot* that originate on the Tree of Life. Various biblical heroes were seen as the living embodiments of their particular *sefirah*. These include: Abraham as *Gedulah,* Isaac as *Din,* Jacob as *Tiferet,* Moses as *Netsach,* Aaron as *Hod,*

Joseph as *Yesod,* and David or the matriarch Rachel as *Malchut* or *Shechinah.* The only soul to descend from *Keter* of the highest world, *Olam Ha-Atzilut,* is the spirit of the Messiah who has yet to come.

The final stamp of our individuality is our acquired personality, known as *Tselem. Tselem* is envisioned as if it were an ethereal body serving as an intermediary between our soul and our physical being. Developed over our entire life as we interact with family, community and environment, our *Tselem* is similar to a "garment" of characteristics and traits which we weave through everything we do. Like a personal intertwining of the two *yetsers,* it is woven not only of the bright side of our virtues but also contains the *Tsel,* the truncated shadow side of those same traits that are our vices. Only the adept were capable of recognizing an individual's *Tselem* and seeing past it to the root of that soul and its place of origin on the *Etz Chayim.*

Just as all reality departed from the One, so will all reality ultimately return to the One. Each human life is a key turning point in that cycle, since each soul can perform *tikkunim.* It can repair fissures in our fragmented world which only that spirit, because of its essence and origin, can perform. Once a soul has completed its task, it ascends to its root *sefirah* on the *Etz Chayim.* When all souls perform their repairs, when all sparks of holiness (*Netsotsot*) have been elevated heavenward, then our fragmented physical existence will be redeemed and transformed back into the seamless spiritual unity of *Echad,* the One God.

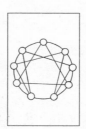

3

The Enneagram

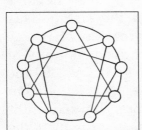 THE TERM ENNEAGRAM IS TAKEN from the Greek and can be translated as "nine points." This starlike diagram has been used to chart the unfolding of both cosmic processes and the human psyche. We might best understand its operation as the joining together of two ancient laws of numerical progression, the Law of the Triad and the Law of the Octave.

Simply stated, the Law of the Triad indicates that every event in our world derives from the interplay of three forces: the active force that initiates a movement; the receptive force that processes that initial action; and the reconciling force that balances the first two so that a new reality might be known. The movement of our world from simple wholeness to its current state of multiplicity might even be seen as a continuing embodiment of the triad law.

In this scenario, Primary Unity, or the One, is split in two in much the way that a single cell organism splits through the biological process of mitosis. The balance needed to creatively harmonize the new relationship of these two is represented by the number three. This process is apparent in the movement from thesis to antithesis to synthesis, in the creative interaction between positive and negative electrical poles, between force and form, between male and female, all of which require a third reconciling factor to bring them such a relationship that a new actuality can come forth.

The Law of the Octave is known to us from music. If a single vibrating string is divided into eight sections by interposing seven frets along it, the change in vibration from one section to the next will increase in a precise mathematical ratio. Although the pitch of each successive note sounds higher, each incrementally shortened segment of string exhibits greater tension, decreased flexibility and less movement than its predecessor. The increasing number of vibrations become more and more densely packed into ever shorter segments of the string. This model was used to describe the progression of reality from the spiritually simple, relaxed and dynamic unity of the divine to the divided, compound, restrained, static coarseness of physical being. The mathematician Francesco Giorgi described this analogy in his sixteenth-century work, *De Harmonia Mundi, On the Harmony of the World*.[8]

Ramon Lull, an occultist who lived in the thirteenth century on Majorca, designed a series of symbolic diagrams in which the number nine represented principles that govern the universe. Drawing upon the earlier work of Giorgi, the Jesuit Athanasius Kircher drew the Ennead in the seventeenth century as three equilateral triangles laid one upon the other (Diagram 3). Each successive triangle represented a descending class of three angels, who were seen in Christianity as intermediaries between God

DIAGRAM 3

and the world.[9] (The three classes of angels are: Seraphim, Cherubim and Thrones; Dominions, Powers and Virtues; Principalities, Archangels and Angels.)

The Armenian-born philosopher George I. Gurdjieff (1877–1949) is credited with introducing the Enneagram to the West. His search for spiritual meaning took him throughout the Middle East and into India. While his writings do not clearly indicate exactly when he learned of the Enneagram, this probably occurred during his travels at the beginning of the twentieth century. Upon returning to Europe he began teaching spirituality and psychology in Moscow and St. Petersburg. He left Russia before the 1919 Revolution, and ultimately migrated near Paris where he opened the Institute for the Harmonious Development of Man.[10]

Unlike Kircher's Enneagram, the diagram taught by Gurdjieff (Diagram 4) has only one self-contained triangle. Gurdjieff compared this enclosed equilateral triangle to the divine, which is perfect but static. The other six points in Gurdjieff's diagram are connected by a line that runs in a sequence of points 1-4-2-8-5-7 and back to point 1. This sequence is based on the recurring decimal that occurs when you divide the number seven, equalling the frets in

DIAGRAM 4

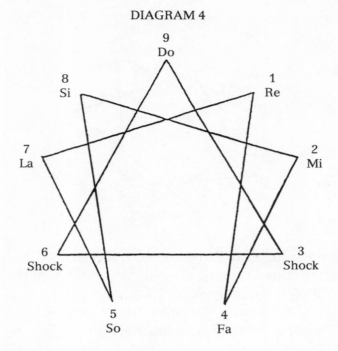

an octave, into One, signifying the original cosmic unity represented by the single vibrating string (i.e. $1 \div 7 = .1428571428571 \ldots$) According to Gurdjieff, this constantly moving pattern represents the dynamic movement of our changing world, with both its continuing rhythms and its need for infusions or shocks of new energy to keep our systems and life from ultimately shutting down.

The recurring decimal pattern connecting the two lower triangles shows the contribution which medieval Islamic mathematics, with its discovery of zero, the decimal system as we know it and these recurring decimals sequences, had upon the Enneagram. Although Gurdjieff attributed the ultimate origin of the symbol to the ancient Sarmoun Brotherhood, it is highly probable that some Sufi orders did transmit to future generations the Enneagram with its Islamic mathematical influences.[11]

Enneagram Theories of Personality

Like the Adam tales, the narrative that underlies the Enneagram theory of personality presupposes both Original
Rightness and a Fall. Each of us is born with our own innate dispositions and an essential trust in our surround-
ings. When we feel at one with the world, we act with
innocence, experiencing no conflicts between our
thoughts, instincts and emotions. Having established no
boundaries, all the potentials of the world are ours.

As a child grows, he or she inevitably experiences the
stresses present in any family situation and the wounds
that come just from living in this material world. To survive, the child develops a separate sense of self, setting
boundaries to protect and defend his essence, particularly
that aspect which she feels is most threatened. Given our
particular combination of temperament and experience, a
filtering of our perspective occurs and almost reflexively
we focus on certain data to protect ourselves where
we feel most vulnerable. Our point of view gradually narrows and our range of options and responses becomes
limited.[12]

The aspect of our idyllic existence which we feel we
have lost, which is that particular aspect of essence that
we feel is most vulnerable, is referred to in Enneagram
terms as our Holy Idea. The mental image that we form of
how to hide our particular weakness is called our Fixation.
Our Passion is that chief emotional trait which arises to
compensate for that element of essence we've lost. Our
Passion which drives the development of our "script," our
pattern of thoughts, feelings and responses that lets us
navigate through life, is known in Enneagram terms as
our Acquired Personality.

In Chapter One, I indicated that the points on the Enneagram represent nine different personality types. Let me
illustrate the process of personality formation by describing how it unfolds for my own personality type: the

Achiever, Point Three. As a very young child, the Three lives with the Holy Idea of Hope that the world is good, that one is loved for who one is and that positive things can occur even when you don't make them happen. Because of a combination of circumstances that might include a demanding family, an unpleasant appearance and a rash temperament, the Three discovers that love and acceptance come not because of who you are, but instead are gained by what you do and how successfully you do it.[13] To compensate, the Three becomes preoccupied with accomplishment and status, with the Fixation of maintaining a winning Image so that others might grant their unstinting approval. The Three's perspective becomes almost instinctively focused on future tasks to perform (the more the better) and how to do these to gain prestige for himself and accolades from others, without which the Three might feel that his world will fall apart.

A Three who is a former professional athlete perfectly described this personality orientation. He stated that during his playing days he was constantly being evaluated by the coaches, the media and the fans. Now, when he does not receive the constant appraisal of others, he feels as if "nothing is going on." Rather than risk the possibility of failure or recrimination, he'll just move on and do something else rather than stay with a task at which he's not doing well. When asked about his feelings, he replied half-jokingly, "We'll get to those later." Even the joy of victory is fleeting to him because "you're always looking forward to the next game." When it was pointed out to him that it seems as if he seeks all his validation from others rather than from inside himself, he simply stated, "external validation, that's my source of survival."[14]

But while compensating for lost Hope, the Three develops a Passion for Deceit. This Passion can manifest itself in portraying an image of being more successful and busy than he really is, of cutting corners to achieve more and of massaging the truth so that a defeat might appear to be a "half victory." Internally, the Three deceives herself by rationalizing shortcomings as being the fault of others or circumstance and dodges her own feelings and inner reflections by moving on to the next task even if the current one is not yet completed. While the Three can be a most effective, enthusiastic leader, he can also be perceived as superficial, if not artificial and concerned more with achieving status than with the sensitivities of others.

Characterizations of Personality

During his lifetime, Gurdjieff did not link his teaching about personality type to the Enneagram symbol. It was Oscar Ichazo, born in 1931, who used his vast knowledge of Western spiritual and philosophical traditions to originate the Enneagram of personality types. The founder of the Arica Institute in Arica, Chile, Ichazo assigned each of the Nine Passions to its appropriate point on the Enneagram. He derived the nine passions by adding two generic passions—fear and deceit—to the seven Deadly Sins first articulated by the Desert Fathers, a group of Christian ascetics who lived in Egypt during the fifth century.[15] Diagram 5 places each of the Nine Passions together with its corresponding fixation at its own Enneagram point.

The following is a short synopsis of each personality type:

Ones: Perfectionists who constantly strive to excel. Seeking to avoid criticism, they become good boys and girls, internalizing their parents' standards while ever monitoring their own behavior for needed improvement. They are idealistic, objective and conscientious, but can display self-righteous anger and be judgmental and rigid with others and themselves. Concerned with order and correctness, they will usually reserve one area of life as a "trap door," a secret activity to release their suppressed chaotic impulses.

DIAGRAM 5
F—Fixation   P—Passion

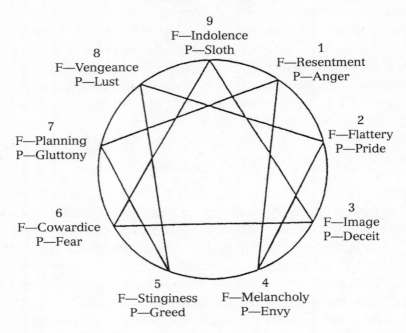

9
F—Indolence
P—Sloth

8
F—Vengeance
P—Lust

1
F—Resentment
P—Anger

7
F—Planning
P—Gluttony

2
F—Flattery
P—Pride

6
F—Cowardice
P—Fear

3
F—Image
P—Deceit

5
F—Stinginess
P—Greed

4
F—Melancholy
P—Envy

Twos: Caregivers. From an early age they learn that their sense of worth depends upon the endorsement of others. Friendly, empathetic and generous, they flatter others for approval and adapt their personality to meet others' desires while ignoring their own. Twos take pride in making themselves indispensable. They manipulate through their helpfulness and become deflated, if not vindictive, when their efforts go unappreciated. Twos often present themselves differently to different people and may keep their friends separate from each other.

Threes: Achievers who work hard for recognition and prestige. To them, achievement ensures love. Energetic, pragmatic and competitive, Threes may sacrifice depth and relationships to attain status and results. Enthusiastic leaders, Threes avoid failure and deceive themselves and others by exaggerating their efforts and "polishing" their defeats to maintain a winning image.

Fours: Romantics. Fashioned by memories of being forsaken by loved ones, Fours seem preoccupied with loss. They focus on the best of what's absent and the deficiencies of what's available. Sensitive, introspective, given to melancholy and shifts of mood, Fours appreciate the artistic and the unique. They avoid the mundane and strive to be perceived as "classy." Living with passionate feelings, Fours envy the lost and the unattainable while drawing their energy from romantic longing.

Fives: Observers who view life from a safe distance. They find the outside world to be intrusive and threatening. Detached, rational and outwardly unemotional, Fives are knowledgeable, insightful and comfortable analyzing abstract ideas, universal principles and group dynamics. Their greed, born from hoarding their ego resources, keeps them from sharing and commitment, while letting them be independent people of modest needs.

Sixes: Because they view the world as a fearful place, they are seen as both Loyalists and Cynics. They look for security in group activities and rules, yet maintain suspicion about the motives of others. The Phobic Six deals with fear by withdrawing from perceived threats and being cautious; the Counter-Phobic Six confronts fear by rushing headlong into challenging situations. Sixes can be wonderful team players, sacrificing heroically for a friend or a mission, while remaining cynical about the intentions of those in charge. Indecisive when insecure, Sixes can fall prey to reactionary movements that offer simple answers to difficult questions, ruthlessly justifying anything for the sake of the cause.

Sevens: Always avoiding pain, these Adventurers hide life's dark side by painting a happy face upon the world. Joyous, spontaneous, possessing a host of interests and abilities, Sevens are gluttons for pleasure. Optimistic, looking to the bright side of present situations and future possibilities, Sevens have trouble with limits and follow-through and may even use alcohol or substance addiction as a refuge from hurt.

Eights: Confrontationists who lust for power and control. To them, respect comes from strength and rejection from weakness. Eights are "bad" boys and girls who seek to dominate situations through confrontation. Assertive, forceful, unsubmitting, Eights learn to respect those who stand up to them and can be strong leaders, especially in the fight against perceived injustice.

Nines: Easy-going, patient and accepting, Nines are Mediators who seek peace by harmonizing differences between others. Seeing others' needs as more important than their own, Nines felt ignored as children and are usually surprised when they are noticed. Nines can appear slothful and lazy because they are not always focused or self-starters and are often ambivalent. Rather than say "no," a Nine might simply not act or become stubborn and passively aggressive. Once having settled on a path, however, Nines can achieve well and be excellent conciliators and counselors because of their humility, simple decisiveness and desire for unity and minimizing conflict.

The Interplay of Triads

We all relate to the world by instinct, by feeling and by thinking. Yet each of us, as a result of our own personalities, emphasize one of these faculties over the other two. The nine personality types are actually set along the Enneagram in three groups of three, each according to its own predominant faculty. These three groups are referred to as the triads.

Points Eight, Nine and One compose the *instinctual triad*. People in this group indicate that they will actually experience bodily sensations when a new situation occurs before they are able to identify what they are thinking or feeling. Because these sensations often are experienced in the abdominal region as "gut feelings," it seems as if the belly has an intelligence of its own. The energy of these "Belly Centered" types is the energy to "stand against," which is manifested by the aggressiveness of the Eight, the stubbornness of the Nine, and the critical perfectionism of the One.

The *feeling triad* is made up of types Two, Three and Four. They are called the "Heart Centered" types because the heart is traditionally seen as the seat of their predominant faculty, the emotions. The energy of these three types seems to move toward others to gauge feelings: the Twos, who wish to be loved; the Threes, who wish to be admired; and the Fours, who wish to be understood.

Five, Six and Seven are the thinking types, the *"Head Centered" triad*. Each of these predominately perceive the world as an intrusive, a fearful, or a limiting place. Their energy seems to move inward: The Five reclusively isolates himself in thought; the Six cautiously pulls back before either escaping from a perceived threat or rushing into it; and the Seven withdraws from current commitment and activities in the ongoing search for new stimulation.

An unusual feature of the Enneagram is that the center type of each triad, located at the three core points on the enclosed triangle, actually appears to repress its triad's own dominant faculty. If the Eight externalizes her instinctual responses by being aggressive and the One internalizes them by becoming self-critical, the Nine seems almost out of touch with instinct and incapable of moving decisively to action. While the Two externalizes emotion so that he can sense even the unspoken needs of others, and the Four internalizes feeling to the extent that he becomes moody and brooding, the Three holds back his feelings lest they interrupt his drive for achievement and success. Similarly, if Fives internalize their thinking to the point of self-isolation and Sevens externalize their thoughts by always planning for exciting future possibilities, the Sixes' thinking can become paralyzed by doubt and thoughts of potential danger that have no connection to reality.

Rather than being the prime example of their triad's predominate faculty, the respective core types might not outwardly show that trait at all. The Nine can seem the least instinctive, the Three the least feeling, and the Six the least thoughtful of all types.

The Dynamics of Types

Our individual personality types are not a static collection of habits and traits. Diagram 6 provides us with a key to understanding how your own type might interact with other types and even assume some of their characteristics.

The circle connecting the points around the circumference indicates the connection which adjacent numbers have to each other. The neighboring numbers on each side of a point are referred to as that point's "Wings." Both

DIAGRAM 6

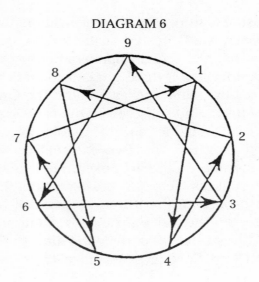

Wings will affect the type, on each side of it, though in every individual one Wing will predominate, giving that personality a distinctive slant. A Two who is a caregiver, for example, might lean either toward the One and be more concerned with order and correctness or toward the Three and be inclined to strive for success to gain recognition and prestige.

Highly important in differentiating personalities within the same type is the use of Instinctual Subtype. As mentioned above, while some of us relate to the world primarily through thinking or feeling, we all possess instincts which help us survive. As with other animals, our survival instincts manifest themselves as three different drives: A drive for self-preservation; a sexual drive that leads to intimacy and propagation of the species; and a social drive to fit in with the group, to maintain the herd. While each of us is sensitive to all three, we are predominantly concerned with the one instinct which is our most vulnerable. This, in turn, will slant how the Fixation and Passion of type will play out for that person in much the same way that a person seated on a three-legged stool will slant if one stool leg is shorter than the other two. Thus, a Two who feels vulnerable in social settings might instinctively turn his attention toward those with power so that he can assure his status in the group. Another Two who is uneasy about establishing intimate relationships might be aggressively flirtatious, while a third Two who is concerned with preserving his own well-being might insist that, since he does so much for others, he should receive preferential treatment.[16]

The arrows along the lines connecting the points to each other represent another sort of interaction among the types. In addition to our predominant type, which determines our conduct during normal circumstances, we tend to move toward another type when under unusual pressure and toward a third when feeling safe and comfortable. The type whose characteristics we assume when we are overwhelmed is called our Stress Point. Movement with the arrow is toward one's Stress Point, such as 1—>4. The movement against the arrow is toward one's Security Point, such as 1<—7. This is the type whose characteristics we exhibit when we feel at great ease. Thus, a One, when facing normal challenges, will exhibit more of the One fixation and become very fussy and picky and concerned with the order and correctness of what he *can* control: My world is falling apart so let me clean this room that I'm in. When facing heavier pressure, she might move to the lower features of her stress point, Four, and feel overly melancholy, maudlin and alienated. When at ease with their companions and environment, Ones can move toward the higher side of their security point, Seven, and be adventurous and playful.[17]

Return to Essence

As mentioned earlier, the Holy Idea indicates that aspect of Essence or original rightness that has been negated. This wounding leads, as we have seen, to the developing of Fixation and Passion as the ways in which the personality compensates for its loss. In the quest for personal growth, one would seek to embody the Virtue that is the opposite of and the balance for one's emotional Passion. Below is a diagram of Essence (Diagram 7) with the Holy Idea above each corresponding Virtue.

While the second half of this book will address the interplay of Essence, Personality and the spiritual task appropriate to each type, let us return for the sake of example to the Three. This type has lost essential Hope that the world is good, that one is loved and that needs are met independent of one's achievement. He fixates on the Vanity of maintaining a winning image and will Deceive others and himself to appear successful and gain accolades and prestige. (See Diagram 5). To achieve spiritual growth and reclaim a measure of his essential lost Hope,

DIAGRAM 7
H.I.—Holy Idea   V—Virtue

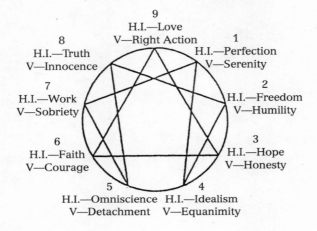

9
H.I.—Love
V—Right Action

8
H.I.—Truth
V—Innocence

1
H.I.—Perfection
V—Serenity

7
H.I.—Work
V—Sobriety

2
H.I.—Freedom
V—Humility

6
H.I.—Faith
V—Courage

3
H.I.—Hope
V—Honesty

5
H.I.—Omniscience
V—Detachment

4
H.I.—Idealism
V—Equanimity

the Three must begin by Honestly examining himself and taking responsibility for his misrepresentations, rationalizations and failures.

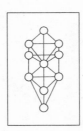

4

Correlation—
Being and Spirit

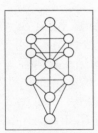 SEVERAL POINTS CONNECT THE KABBAL-
istic system of the *sefirot* and the Enneagram,
especially since theories of being in both
begin with an Essential One which unfolds
into multiple characteristics. Both the
ten-aspect Tree of Life and the nine-pointed
Enneagram posit dynamic internal interaction
within the system—what Gurdjieff called "perpetual motion" and Kabbalah terms *Ratso Vashov,* "Egress and
Return."

In the realm of personality, both the Enneagram and
Kabbalah claim that although all psyches potentially embody all the potencies, each manifests a predominant type
or derives from a particular *sefirah.* Just as the Enneagram
speaks of an acquired personality with its interrelated
light and dark sides, so does Kabbalah describe the *Tselem,* the ethereal "garment" of our traits and experiences

which we develop over our lifetime, which inevitably includes its truncated shadow side or *Tsel*. Just as Kabbalah divides our souls into *Nefesh, Ruah* and *Neshama,* the Enneagram also details three centers of intelligence: the Belly, which is instinctually concerned with our physical survival; the Heart, which is our emotional core; and the Head, which is our mental center.

Finally, in both systems there is a shattering of the whole and a restorative, redemptive process. Kabbalah speaks of *Shevirat Ha Kelim,* the shattering of the seven lower *sefirot* because they could not successfully contain the *Shefa,* the radiant energy of *Ayn Sof.* It also speaks about how *Netsotsot,* the sparks of that divine radiance, were scattered throughout the world. It is the task of each individual to elevate the *Netsotsot* of our own *sefirah* so that these sparks—and ultimately each individual's soul— might return to its rightful home in the Tree of Life. The Enneagram speaks of a more personal shattering, first in childhood when we lose that aspect of Essence which is our Holy Idea, and later when we mature and, because of a loss or a setback or an illness or just during a moment of realization, we realize how stifling are our habits and rationalizations. (Perhaps the rabbinic proscription to refrain from studying Kabbalah until age 40 was not merely to address the student's need for mature stability, but to give the seeker a chance to acquire the existential openness that only comes from life's brokenness and examining our values and goals in middle age.) By moving from our Fixation and its corresponding Passion toward our Virtue, we can reconnect with the Holy Idea of Essence and feel that we are at home with existence.

In his book, *In Search of the Miraculous,* P. D. Ouspensky records Gurdjieff as referring to a book entitled *Merkhavat*. While *Merkavah* ("Chariot") is the name of the earliest movement in the Jewish mysticism, there is no known book entitled *Merkhavat*. Ichazzo asserted his own ties to Jewish mysticism by claiming that the archangel Metatron revealed to him the placement of the Passions.[18]

Points of Juncture

Although these passing references obscure as much as they reveal, common influences on the Kabbalah and the Enneagram derive from antiquity and medieval times. These include Pythagoreanism, Neoplatonism, Gnosticism, Christian Asceticism and Sufism.[19] An early attempt to place the *sefirot* along the points of the Enneagram was attempted in the seventeenth century by the aforementioned Athanasius Kircher. He located three *sefirot* (*Keter, Chochmah, Binah; Gedulah, Din, Tiferet; Netsach, Hod, Yesod*) along the three self-contained triangles overlaid one on the other (Diagram 8).

When Gurdjieff opened the Enneagram's bottom two triads, the three highest *sefirot* remained at the points of the self-contained triangle. The lower six were placed along the two open, interconnected triads representing their dynamic interaction. (Diagram 9) The circle joining the points symbolized *Malchut, Shechinah,* the tenth *sefirah,* representing God's Presence, which encircles the world.

DIAGRAM 8

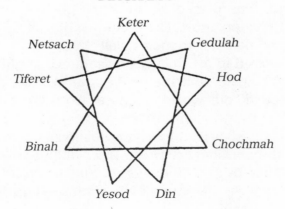

DIAGRAM 9

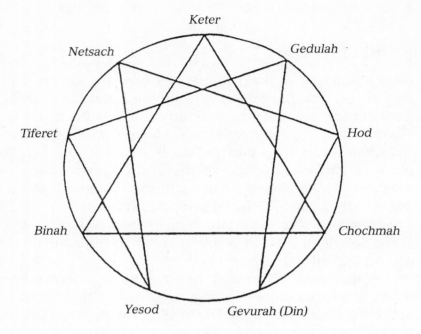

When I first saw this placement of the *sefirot* along the Enneagram, it seemed somewhat out of order: *Keter,* which is the point of transition from potential to actuality, was occupying the mediating, accepting Nine point. *Yesod,* representing the assertive force of the male generative organ, was placed in the introspective, emotionally detached Five position. The configuration of the other *sefirot* seemed peculiar to me as well.

It occurred to me that this dissonance might be traced to the Kabbalistic doctrine of the four worlds. According to this doctrine our world emanates from *Ayn Sof* through four descending realms of increasing physical density. Each world has, as its underlying reality, its own representation of the *Etz Chayim.* These Trees of Life are connected to each other by the final *sefirah, Shechinah,* of the prior Tree serving as the *Keter* of the succeeding Tree. (The relationship between these two *sefirot* is further alluded to in their names: *Keter,* "Crown," and *Malchut,* "Sovereignty." In some Kabbalistic schema, the final *sefirah* is even called *Atarah,* "Tiara.") Therefore, it would make sense that in the realm governing human personality, the fourth world (*Olam Ha-asiya*), *Shechinah* would occupy the top position on the Enneagram.

The placement of *Shechinah* rather than *Keter* at the top position is supported by two additional facts. Since only the Messiah's soul will derive from *Keter,* no single human personality type can be rooted in that *sefirah.* Additionally, *Shechinah* accepts and harmonizes the divine energy from the other *sefirot* in the same way that Nines accept and harmonize others' divergent points of view.

By beginning with *Shechinah* in the Nine position, Diagram 10 seems to me to be the most valid placement of the *sefirot* along the Enneagram.

The above configuration places *Keter* in the middle, hovering above the diagram as the transition from the

DIAGRAM 10

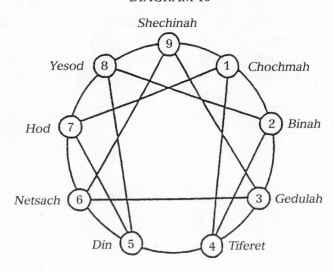

One to the many. The other nine *sefirot* now seem to correlate more readily to the Enneagram types:

1. *Chochmah*—The all-knowing, Correct, Internalized Father, *Abba*.

2. *Binah*—The understanding, Controlling, Supernal Mother, *Ima*.

3. *Gedulah*—Impetus to be great.

4. *Tiferet*—Beauty, and Romantic Longing.

5. *Din*—Bound, Enclosed, Limited.

6. *Netsach*—Enduring, and Seeking Authority.

7. *Hod*—Splendor

8. *Yesod*—Seminal Force.

9. *Shechinah*—Accepting Presence.

Because *Din* and *Tiferet* are usually numbered four and five on lists of the *sefirot,* attempts have been made to correlate *Din* to Point Four and *Tiferet* to Point Five. As I mentioned above and will detail in the following chapters, I believe that *Tiferet* more closely corresponds to the traits of Point Four, the Romantic, and *Din* to Point Five, the Observer. Conceptually, the reason for this reversal might be Gurdjieff's opening of the Enneagram's lower two triangles (see Diagrams 3 and 4), a configuration that flipped the positions of Points Four and Five, the bottom two points on the Enneagram.[20]

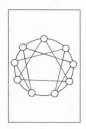

The Enneagram through the Lens of Kabbalah

5

The Sefirot: *Type and Redemption through Spiritual Task*

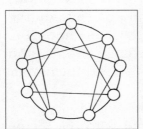 RELIGIONS CLASSICALLY DEPICT saints and sinners as having fairly specific virtues or vices. Judaism is no different. It traditionally speaks of three categories of individuals: the *Tsadik,* or Righteous; the *Rashah,* or Wicked; and all the rest of us, the *Benoni,* which literally means, "those hovering in the middle." A powerful insight of the Enneagram is that these categories manifest themselves as levels of development for each type. The vices at the low level of a Point's development are the compulsions or *Sitra Achra,* the "Other Side" of the virtues found at their higher level.[1]

In this section, we will examine each *Sefirah*/Enneagram Point. In the first paragraph of each chapter, we will set forth in bold type the names of the types, their specific *Shevirah,* "Shattering," or the basic premise of their fall from Essence or Holy Idea into the Fixation and Passion of Acquired Personality and how these manifest in the three *Subtypes*. We will then consider what a *Rashah* (an unredeemed), a *Benoni* (an average) and a *Tsadik* (a redeemed exemplar) of each type might be. To illustrate these Points, we will look at the profiles of those scriptural figures whom the Kabbalah considered to be the embodiments of their particular type. Since we all fluctuate between the various levels of development, we will observe this movement in the triumphs and pitfalls of the various Biblical heroes.

For those wishing to begin or renew their Jewish observance, each chapter will suggest a different Gateway or *Sha'ar*. As a result of their special orientations, each of these activities will have a stronger appeal for each Enneagram type. An observance or ritual that might prove particularly appealing to each type will be described for those seeking to connect or reconnect with Jewish life.

Also, a variety of different approaches have been prescribed for students of the Enneagram who seek serious personal growth. Among them are trying to embody the Virtue of your type, confronting and dwelling upon the characteristics which your type instinctually avoids, and trying to shift your style of behavior to manifest the higher traits of your Security Point.

To again return to our Three, if she wishes to grow she might balance her Passion for Deceit with the Virtue of Honesty by being fully truthful with others and by ruthlessly examining her feelings and her own self-deceptions. If, because of her overwhelming need to succeed, she avoids all association with failure, she must then claim responsibility for her defeats and live with their repercussions rather than portray them as partial victories or blame them on circumstances or on other people. Finally, our Three might try to exhibit the higher traits of her Security Point, Type Six, to cooperate rather than always compete with others and to show constancy in her allegiances rather than constantly shift around for the sake of expediency.

The Wisdom of Cordevero

The spiritual disciplines listed as *Tikkun*/Repair at the end of the following chapters are taken from *Tomer Devorah,* or *Deborah's Palm Tree,* written by Rabbi Moshe Cordevero and first published in Venice in 1587.[2] Cordevero, who lived in Safed in Northern Israel in the sixteenth century, was a student of the great mystical legalist Rabbi Joseph Caro. He also taught the seminal Kabbalist, Rabbi Isaac Luria.

The spiritual tasks which Cordevero sets forth have two goals. The first is to help us identify with and embody the qualities found in each of the *sefirot.* As such, his disciplines lead students to manifest the *Virtue* of the given *sefirah:* sometimes by emulation; sometimes by a task that makes them confront their avoidance; and sometimes by acts that exhibit the higher qualities of their Security Point. These very concrete acts are consistent with the traditional rabbinic prescription *"Lo Hamidrash Haikar Elah Hamaoseh . . . ,"* "It is the deed and not the exposition which is essential."

Cordevero's disciplines have a second, more sublime purpose. To understand this goal better, let us revisit the *Etz Chayim* of Diagram 1.

According to Kabbalistic thought, Adam's Fall produced severe dislocations in the Tree of Life and, therefore, in the world. The pathways that convey the *Shefa,* the divine radiance, from *Ayn Sof* to the various *sefirot* have become misaligned, if not completely severed. *Shechinah* is in exile, cut off from the rest of the Tree. Her connection along the center pathways to *Tiferet* and *Yesod,* and their connection to each other, has been weakened and stretched. The full measure of divine energy cannot flow through the center pathways to our world below. The

DIAGRAM 1

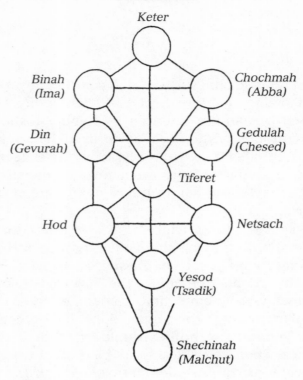

Keter

Binah (Ima)

Chochmah (Abba)

Din (Gevurah)

Gedulah (Chesed)

Tiferet

Hod

Netsach

Yesod (Tsadik)

Shechinah (Malchut)

forces of the Left side are out of balance with those on the Right. This causes a predominance of *Din*'s harsh judgments because they are not properly tempered with the mercy of *Chesed*. These blocks to the proper flow of *Shefa* to the individual *sefirot* also means that during this unredeemed time, the *sefirot* themselves will exhibit lower as well as higher traits.

Because each of us is created in God's image, what we do on earth resonates in the divine sphere above. Therefore, the tasks that Cordevero detailed perform the function of *Tikkun,* of bringing needed repair to the *Etz Chayim* and the individual *sefirot*. As such, our own spiritual quest can lead us not only to self-growth, but to divine repair and world redemption.

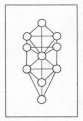

6

Point One: Chochmah—*Wisdom*

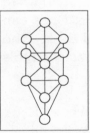THOSE WHO OCCUPY POINT ONE ON the Enneagram are usually viewed as **Perfectionists**. By perceiving the world as a place that criticizes and penalizes wrong thought and deed, Ones have lost the Holy Idea of **Perfection**, the undivided rightness of all things. Having learned that approval comes from correcting error and being good, Ones develop a mental fixation of **Resentment** and an emotional passion of **Anger**. They deny their own desires in the face of exacting internal and external standards. On the instinctual Subtype level, the passion can manifest itself as **Jealousy**, the critical judging of one's mate's intentions in intimate situations; as **Inadaptability** in social settings; and as the **Anxiety** that comes from making a mistake and endangering one's self-preservation.

Corresponding to Point One is the *sefirah* of

Chochmah, or Wisdom. The critical nature of the One makes this Kabbalistic attribution quite fitting, since Ones can give the impression that only they have wisdom to know fully what is correct in every situation.

PERSONALITY AND ITS LEVELS

Given their abiding commitment to principle, Ones tend to be conscientious, honest, hard-working and responsible. They value integrity, punctuality and precision in themselves and others. Always concerned with "doing the right thing," Ones strive for excellence and constantly seek ways to improve themselves and others. Their high moral sense can lead them to crusade for justice and truth.

Because of their temperament and upbringing, Ones are quite self-critical but have a hard time accepting criticism from others. They displace their anger by finding fault with those who violate conventional standards, and who seem to be "getting away with something." By cloaking their anger in moral self-righteousness, Ones can avoid the inner recriminations that come from having bad feelings toward others. At their most obsessive, Ones can be dogmatic, inflexible and even cruel toward those who don't do what they know is right. Ones have described this orientation as:

> "I never feel acceptable so I strive to be perfect so I won't be cast aside . . ." "The search for security lies in getting things right . . ." "Error gets you expelled from the Garden [of Eden] and brings down the hierarchy of the world."

Ones inhabit a world of mental comparisons: Do my actions and thoughts live up to my ideal? Are others criticizing me? Is someone else ahead of me? Will I feel diminished if I compliment someone else? Caught between their desires and their sense of "should," Ones may procrastinate, wavering between doing what they want to do, which might not be correct, and doing what is correct, which isn't really what they want. Seeking what might be termed as "trapdoor release," Ones can develop a dual self. They can be proper at home, while playful on holiday, or have a meticulously clean desk top, but reserve one drawer for clutter and junk. Prim and proper, some Ones actually vacation far from home so that they can sunbathe undetected by friends or acquaintances at nude beaches.

As with all personality types, Ones display different levels of development. The *Tsadik* or redeemed One is wise, conscientious, has great integrity and principles and is willing to fight for justice and truth. The *Benoni,* or moderately developed person, values protocol, etiquette and rules, and criticizes, moralizes and tries to improve everyone else. A *Rashah,* or unredeemed One, is intolerant, punitive and condescendingly self-righteous, sees absolutes with no shades of grey, and treats others' mistakes as heinous crimes while becoming paralyzed by his own quest for perfection.

THE BIBLICAL HERO: *ABBA*
Kabbalists personified the *sefirah* of *Chochmah* as *Abba,* Supernal Father. In many ways, Ones seem to respond to the internalized voice of an ascendant father. This inner voice continually calls them to perfection, to do better. In effect, it states, "You'll be loved if you deserve it, if you're right."

On a conceptual basis, *Chochmah* is much like the Essence of Perfection—it contains the undifferentiated, pristine ideals of all that exists. However, when in character fixation, the One's perception mimics Essence by angrily looking to the correctibility of things. Their penchant for criticism comes from measuring our flawed actuality against the yardstick of their conceived, but unrealized, ideals. "Oh, how perfect this could be" gives way to "Damn! How lacking this really is." Interestingly, Kabbalists have identified *Chochmah* with "Yod," the first

Hebrew letter of God's four-letter name (YHWH). Yod looks just like a point (ʸ) that geometrically has the potential for expansion in all three dimensions. *Chochmah*, like the point, contains the possibility for measuring and, thus, comparing all things. Organically, *Chochmah* is likened to a seed that contains all the biological information needed for the new life. However, *Chochmah* truly becomes *Abba*, "Father," only when it engenders and identifies with all life, accepting in wholeness the beauty and the flaws of that which exists.

SHA'AR/GATEWAY

Justice and righteousness are key Jewish values. The High Holy Day liturgy describes God as a "Just King" who is exalted by righteousness. The words of Isaiah, which are read on Yom Kippur, proclaim, "loose the bonds of wickedness . . . and let the oppressed go free." *Aleynu*, the prayer of adoration, bids us to join in this task so that we might "perfect the world under the kingship of God."

These calls to justice and social reform match the Ones' dedication to principle and quest to improve the world around them. High Holy Day worship can remind them that such striving is godly when motivated by righteous concern for others rather than by self-righteousness. Throughout the year, they can help "perfect the world" by joining with Jewish and interfaith groups whose religious principles lead them to work for a more equitable and just society.

Rosh Hashanah and Yom Kippur call each of us to examine our motivations and our deeds. While self-evaluation comes naturally to Ones, the Holy Days stress that we should undertake such activity for the sake of reconciliation and atonement. By emphasizing the urgency and frailty of human existence the Holy Days teach Ones, and all of us, that life is too short to harbor resentment. Each day of each new year is the time to admit when you are wrong, to seek the forgiveness of people we've hurt and to forgive those who have hurt us.

TIKKUN/REPAIR

In the third chapter of his *Tomer Devorah*, Cordevero addresses the path of growth associated with *Chochmah*: "How should one act to become accustomed to the divine quality of *Chochmah* . . . be ready to give beneficial teaching to all, to each according to that individual's ability to understand."

Ones who seek further spiritual growth must begin by softening the harshness of their principles and standards by recognizing that positive change can only come when you teach others for their benefit, not when you criticize them to enhance your own feelings of validation.

If Anger is the Passion of Ones, then *Serenity* is One's Virtue. To achieve serenity, Cordevero counsels daily time for each of us to be engaged in "contemplation in solitude upon [his] Creator." In that way, wisdom can be realized by calming the passions and acknowledging that perfection lies only with God and not in unattainable absolutes. The divine balancing of judgment with compassion, of life's expansive and constricting traits, is how Ones, and all others, can achieve wholeness.

The Enneagram indicates that One's Security Point is Seven, the point of joy and vitality. Cordevero calls Ones to embrace the higher traits of vivaciousness "to teach life to the world . . . [to] spout forth life toward all things." If Ones are judgmental and disdain the unconventional while seeking only stable "worthwhile" companions, Cordevero encourages them to "bring back the outcasts and think only good concerning them."

In their highest manifestations as *Tsadik*, Ones can be idealistic reformers whose principled, uncondescending stands lead them to fight for truth and justice. Thus, Cordevero writes:

He should always seek mercy and blessings for all creatures.

He ought to petition constantly for their deliverance from oppression . . .

He will think of those who are cut off, seek out the needs of the young, heal those that are broken; feed the needy and return the strayed ones . . . let him not hold himself aloof or find such tasks debasing; but let him lead as each requires to be led.

For Cordevero, the result of these actions is to bring the Ones not only to good conduct but to a unique identification with *Chochmah* which will help restore its proper influence upon the divine and our world. "He will be led . . . into Righteousness in Upper Thought (*Chochmah*) which guides *Adam Kadmon* aright." (This is the *sefirot* configured as Primordial Man. See Chapter 2 for more details.)

7

Point Two:
Binah—Understanding

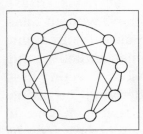 OF THE VARIOUS ENNEAGRAM
types, Twos are deemed to be the
Caregivers. Having lost the Holy Idea
of **Freedom**, that their needs will be
met without having always to manipulate or serve others, Twos have learned
that to receive you must give. They
develop a mental fixation of **Flattery**, which they use
to charm other people. They also develop the emotional
passion of **Pride**, which makes them feel indispensable
to those whom they help. Instinctually, the Two's Subtypes
are aggressively **Seductive** in intimate situations; **Ambi-
tious** to secure the attention and prestige of being associated with powerful people in social situations; they feel
that, because they give so much, they have the right
to a "Me First" privilege in the preserving of their own
well-being.

It is not coincidental that the *sefirah* that correlates to the Two is *Binah*. This *sefirah* embodies understanding, which is a core trait of the Two. Twos can intuitively sense the special needs of others and offer them just the help they require. So, too, does *Binah* allot to each of the succeeding seven *sefirot* of the *Etz Chayim* that aspect of *shefa,* the radiant energy, that it needs to manifest its own unique divine trait.

PERSONALITY AND ITS LEVELS

Motivated by a need to be needed, Twos tend to be loving and supportive. Desiring both physical and emotional closeness, Twos can remain strongly committed to relationships in which they feel wanted. Appearing altruistic to a fault, they can give great amounts of their time and energy to others. "No" is a hard word for a Two to say. In groups, Twos make everyone feel welcome, aid others in their tasks and are sensitive to how shared decisions effect everyone involved.

However, this seeming selflessness can mask an assumption that others can accomplish nothing without their indispensable aid. When their efforts go unrecognized and their love unreturned, Twos can become vindictive and move from portraying themselves as saviors to acting first as victims and then as persecutors. Underlying the giving nature of the Two is a certain manipulative dynamic. If love and security can be gained by meeting the needs of others, then the Two will do this. Control can be achieved by being helpful and making themselves indispensable— and then pointing out how much others are indebted to them. Twos describe this manipulation in this way:

> "I'm the one who can help. I'm indispensable. It's a prideful stance, manipulative and invasive." "I have a real sense that only I can do it. This is a compulsion to help others, and thereby, to get my own needs met indirectly."

Often, Twos will attach themselves to powerful people so they can bask in the reflected glory of being invaluable to those with undeniable status. Such people have the power and influence to ensure that the Twos' desires are met. While growing up, Twos were loved when they pleased others. As such, their sense of worth developed in response to how others reacted to them. They learned to adapt their personality to fit the desires of others and to read others' emotional states through their smiles, frowns, gestures and expressions. But being so other-directed made them lose touch with their own needs. They wonder if they are really loving or playing a role of how a loving person should act. Tensions can develop between the Two's desire to merge with his or her partner and a strong conflicting desire to break free.

Twos can be quite flirtatious and seek sexual attention as a sign of approval. But even more than sex, they want to know that they're wanted even if they aren't sure that they want the object of their flirtations. Twos are most energized when moving toward challenging relationships, being attracted to attached partners not to hurt the partner's spouse, but to overcome the hurdle of that partner's unavailability. True intimacy, however, can threaten the Two because it might expose the fact that there is no real self inside them.

At the redeemed level of *Tsadik,* Twos can be compassionate, empathic, forgiving and sincere. They can display a deep commitment to help others be their best without thinking of personal gain. Moderately developed as a *Benoni,* Twos can be overly friendly and flattering, cloyingly co-dependent in their need to be needed, imposing themselves on others so as not to be abandoned while playing the martyr to prove their own worth. A *Rashah,* or an unredeemed Two, can be manipulative, histrionic and self-serving. Twos might abuse people, food and substances to mask their feelings of being unappreciated, and instill guilt in others and act as their custodians to bind people to them.

THE BIBLICAL HEROINE: *IMA*

Whether male or female, Twos are often noted for their mothering qualities. Their pride mimics their lost Essence of Freedom, which spurs them to think they can fulfill all needs. Functioning in a healthy manner, Twos are nurturing enablers. When caught in an unhealthy state, they are possessive and smothering. Kabbalists have personified the corresponding *sefirah, Binah,* as the Supernal Mother, *Ima.* If *Chochmah* is portrayed as a seed, then *Binah* is the womb into which the seed is implanted. All individualization takes place therein and ultimately all the other seven *sefirot* emerge from *Ima.*

Like the Two, in fixation, there is a controlling aspect to *Ima.* As the Well or Fountain of Blessing, it is *Ima* who continues to nourish and sustain each of her sefirotic offspring even after they have emerged from her. Just as the Two offers different aspects of his or her personality to different people, so does *Ima* mediate her divine energy through different paths to each *sefirah.*

While maintaining an attachment to the other *sefirot, Ima* looks forward to the time of *Hitball'ut,* Cosmic Reintegration, when her sefirotic children will return to her. However, rather than shackling or smothering them, that return will be the ultimate Sabbath and Jubilee. *Ima* will enable each *sefirah* to go out to freedom and ascend to its own essential higher state as part of *Ayn Sof.*

SHA'AR/GATEWAY

In *Pirke Avot,* the *Ethics of the Fathers,* deeds of loving kindness are listed with worship and Torah study as one of three pillars upon which the world stands.

Each morning, at the very beginning of the synagogue liturgy, worshippers recite a list of these loving acts, which are known in Hebrew as *Gemilut Hasadim.*

They include providing hospitality to travelers, visiting the sick, ensuring that the indigent have the means to marry and showing proper respect to the deceased both by attending funerals and by consoling the bereaved. These deeds are considered so important that those who perform them are rewarded in this world and throughout eternity.

Given the Twos' inclination towards helpfulness, these activities might provide an appropriate starting point for their Jewish involvement. Working with committees that help comfort the bereaved and assisting the ill and the needy seems a natural way for Twos to use their talents and find a place within the Jewish community.

Through prayer and study of sacred texts, Twos and others can learn that these loving acts are more than good deeds or ways to gain self-validation through helpfulness. Judaism actually views them as ways of imitating God. Scripture bids us to "walk after God" and Israel's sages tell us the way to do that is "to be compassionate as God is compassionate." Reciting prayers each day like Psalms 145 and 146 remind us that God's dreams for the world include feeding the hungry and helping those who are vulnerable and dispossessed. By performing these and other loving acts, we become partners in making God's dreams become real.

TIKKUN/REPAIR

Afflicted with the Passion of pride, Twos need to develop the virtue of Humility as a path back to Essence. To do so, Cordevero recommends in *Tomer Devorah* the spiritual discipline of *Teshuvah,* or Repentance:

> How should one train in the quality of *Binah*?
>   By Repentance, for there is nothing so worthy . . . *Binah* tempers judgments and destroys their bitterness . . . return in true penitence and correct every imperfection.

At first glance, it would appear strange that a caring, giving Two would need to repent. Yet each of the three stages of repentance can be beneficial to the Two.

The first step, *Vidui,* is that of confession. Rather than inflate one's importance to others or exhibit false modesty, the Two needs to recognize and admit his real worth and his own real needs. This confronting of who one is without the false tendencies of self-exaltation or debasement is the beginning of real humility. This can also lead to admitting that manipulation and control can often be the motive behind the Twos' helpfulness. In this way, Twos can move toward the higher qualities of their security point, Four, and begin to recognize their own true emotions and needs.

Tefillah, or prayer, is the second stage of repentance. For those who see all help emanating from them, prayer can be beneficial in asking for divine assistance and in cultivating humility. Not only can prayer provide insight, but it can disabuse Twos of the illusion that everyone needs them while they don't need anyone.

The final act of Repentance is performing loving, charitable deeds. These are known as *tsedakah,* whose root is *tsedek,* righteousness. *Tikkun* can be achieved if one now offers care and nurture not as a way to control others or for self-validation, but simply because it is right. As Cordevero wrote:

> If you do well you can root yourself in the mystery of repentance, converting formerly evil deeds to their root in the mystery of the good . . . accusers . . . are converted into good sponsors. . . . Thus one cleanses the harmful inclination (*Yetser HaRa*), brings it into the region of the beneficial (*Yetser Ha Tov*), and replants him in holiness.

The literal meaning of the Hebrew word for repentance, *teshuvah,* is "return." This is the same word used to describe the ultimate return of the seven succeeding *sefirot* to *Binah*. Perhaps the lesson for Twos is that cloying and control will not prevent others from abandoning you. Only by freely giving care can you ensure that others will want to return in friendship to you. And through repentance, the redeemed Two can hasten *Hitball'ut,* the time of Cosmic Reintegration into Essence. As Cordevero writes, "Whoever lives all his days with thoughts of repentance causes understanding (*Binah*) to shine upon all his days . . . and the days of his life are crowned."

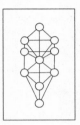

8

Point Three:
Gedulah—*Greatness*

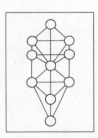 THREES HAVE BEEN ALTERNATIVELY called **Succeeders, Achievers** or **Performers**. Having lost the Essential state of **Hope** that good things can occur, independent of their efforts, Threes learn to gain approval through achievement. Preoccupied with the fixation of **Vanity** in maintaining a winning **Image**, the Threes' passion for **Deceit** can lead to "polishing" defeats and portraying themselves as more accomplished or prestigious than they really are. Instinctually, Threes who are in intimate relationships strive to present themselves to their partners as embodying the ideal **Image** of a male and female, pursue **Prestige** and status in social groups and seek material **Security** as a sign of self-worth in the area of self-preservation.

Gedulah, or greatness, is the *sefirah* which corresponds to Point Three. *Gedulah* is the expansive grace of

God's loving power. Portrayed in the imagery of *Adam Kadmon, Gedulah* is God's strong right arm.

PERSONALITY AND ITS LEVELS

Threes occupy the core point of the Enneagram's feeling or heart triad. Twos want to be loved by others. Fours want to be understood by others. Threes want to be admired by others.

If Threes have a motto, it is "You are what you produce." Having been prized for what they achieved, Threes compete well for personal victory or to rally their team. Threes can become the exemplars of the highest ideals of those groups they deem significant. As masters of promotion, Threes can move directly from an idea into action. Using activity as a way to avoid depression, they keep full schedules and always have several balls in the air.

Because appearing successful is of ultimate importance to them, Threes fool themselves and others about how successful or how busy they really are. They may abandon faltering projects before a failure occurs or blame can be assigned. Authenticity and depth can be sacrificed for superficiality as long as the status is high, the title is right and the check has enough zeroes.

There is a chameleonlike quality about Threes that lets them change their personae to fit the ideal of each group with which they are involved. Experts at advancing themselves, Threes are vain about their importance to a project. Concerned with personal status, they play to win and seek positions of authority and power over others.

Threes describe their approach to image and competition this way:

> "Image needs to be present all the time, whether it's appearing as a corporate executive, a biker or as a member of the society horse set. It seems like I'm doing what I need to do and I'm not really practicing a

form of deceit." "I'm going to win. If I don't, I'll ratio-
nalize that I've won some way."

Threes prefer to associate with those who are accomplished and attractive and usually remain close to others
only when they are engaged in a project or social activity.
When romantically involved, Threes may project the
image of an ideal, sensitive lover while expressing feelings
that don't really correspond to their true emotions. During
a moment of great intimacy, their attention may shift else-
where.

At the *Tsadik* level, Threes are energetic, resourceful
and self-assured. Their infectious enthusiasm and unquali-
fied commitment may support worthy goals and the projects of others. Moderately developed *Benoni* Threes can
be social climbing chameleons and project whatever
image will gain the most admiration. Their obsession with
accomplishment and competition can lead them to look
down on others. As a *Rashah,* Threes are hollow, vain and
pretentious, and are so fearful of failure that they will lie,
cheat and betray others to maintain their self-image.

THE BIBLICAL HERO: ABRAHAM

Kabbalists have viewed the Biblical figure of Abraham as
the incarnation of *Gedulah.* The tales about Abraham reveal that he shared many of the higher and some of the
baser characteristics of the Three. Although the Torah tells
nothing of Abraham's childhood, rabbinic lore indicates
that great achievements were expected from him even before his birth.

God lured Abraham to his mission with three
promises: Abraham would become a mighty nation, he
would receive material blessings and he would achieve a
great reputation. Obviously, God knew Abraham well because the possibility of success, prosperity and a grand
image spurred Abraham to leave Mesopotamia for Canaan.
Fearing that he might be killed so that someone else could

take his wife, Abraham twice falsely introduced Sarah as his sister, once to Pharaoh (Genesis 12:13) and once to the Philistine King Avimelech (Genesis 20:2). The result of each charade was the enrichment of Abraham's family.

An effective, forceful leader, Abraham formed a successful alliance following the defeat and enslavement of Sodom by the King of Elam, Chedarlaomer. Abraham freed the captives, including his own nephew, Lot. Yet even at his altruistic best, when he refused personal gain from his victory, Abraham exhibited a lingering concern with image, declaring, "Let no one say 'I have enriched Abraham'" (Genesis 14:23).

Despite these foibles, there were moments when Abraham became the paradigm of the human ideal and the best a person could be. When confronted with the impending destruction of Sodom, Abraham argued with God that the righteous might be killed unfairly with the wicked (Genesis 18:25). Before concluding a political alliance with Avimelech, Abraham delayed negotiations until the Philistine ruler clarified a matter of stolen wells even though Abraham himself might not have been among the injured parties (Genesis 21:25). Even in the midst of his most terrifying mission, the abortive sacrifice of Isaac at Mount Moriah, Abraham was able to say three times *"Hineni,* I am here and fully present"—in response to God, to his child Isaac and finally to the angelic call which bade him to refrain from harm and stay his hand (Genesis 22). And finally, despite his image as a mighty prince of God, Abraham personally attended to the details of Sarah's funeral by purchasing her burial plot at an exorbitant fee, eulogizing her, weeping openly and burying her with his own hands (Genesis 23). For these reasons, the prophet Isaiah considered Abraham worthy of the title "God's Friend."

SHA'AR/GATEWAY

Although Judaism has a rich philosophic tradition, its greatest emphasis is on action. This orientation is summed

up by the previously quoted statement that it is not the exposition but the deed which is essential. Rather than having long lists of dogmas, Judaism is centered around
performing *mitzvot,* divine commandments that prescribe
how every aspect of our lives can be sanctified by specific
acts. These range from worship to the observance of dietary laws to business ethics.

This pragmatic approach should prove appealing to
Threes, who are not inclined toward ongoing introspec-
tion. The realization that God can be served by concrete
acts that have practical rationale can provide Threes with
a comfortable entrée into Jewish life. The idea of being
validated by what you *do* corresponds to the orientation
of the Three.

Within Jewish life, there are ample opportunities for
those, like Threes, who wish to assume leadership roles.
From congregational committees and boards to leading
services and reading scripture to involvement in charitable and Zionist enterprises, there are numerous chances to
step forward, do needed work and receive recognition.
However, the Hebrew terms for doing community work,
Tsorchai Tsibbur, and leading in worship, *Shaliach Tsibbur,*
literally mean meeting the "needs of the community" and
being the "messenger of the community." Both phrases remind Threes and everyone else that the distinction that
accompanies such godly work is not for personal aggran-
dizement, but for the common good.

TIKKUN/REPAIR

The virtue of the Threes is *Honesty.* To achieve this state,
Cordevero in *Tomer Devorah* recommends immersing
ourselves in the love of God. This avoids the unceasing
pursuit of status, worldly gain and a winning image, and
provides a transcendent constancy:

> The main entry . . . is by way of utter love of the Lord
> which he will not desert for any cause . . . it behooves

one to first arrange for the needs of divine worship and . . . [then] look to his other needs. The love of God should be fixed in his heart regardless of whether he receives bounty or suffering.

In the Bible, the foreskin represented whatever obstructs our true generative powers. It metaphorically blocks truth and God's word from penetrating our heart. Drawing on this imagery, Cordevero instructs that:

. . . every action must be performed properly . . . and every semblance of husk or foreskin must be removed. Every cause which produced this foreskin must be pursued . . . in such a manner . . . he cuts away the foreskin from his own heart causing the righteous to be without husk.

Rather than social climbing and appearing only in the company of the attractive and the accomplished, Cordevero prescribes performing the following acts to be a human paradigm: visiting and healing the sick, giving donations to the poor, providing hospitality for the homeless, dowering indigent brides and making peace with others. These acts come naturally for Twos and can be their entry point into Judaism. For Threes, they serve a different purpose. They highlight the *Chesed* of *Gedulah,* the dedicated kindness inherent in true greatness, and move Threes toward the higher qualities of Security Point Six where loyalty and commitment to others temper self-promotion.

When performed with *kavannah,* proper intention, the disciplines described above not only assure the Threes' real attainments in this world, they trigger cosmic ramifications as well. By acting kindly, by taking responsibility for one's defeats and setbacks in life and by trying to derive lessons about personal goodness from them, Threes can balance *Din'*s limitations, which is located on the Left side of the *Etz Chayim* with the kind fullness of the Right

side's *Chesed*. These acts can strengthen the proper align-
ment of *Tiferet, Yesod* and *Malchut* along the Center pathways, bringing the flow of *Ayn Sof's* light to the spheres
below.

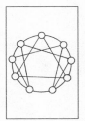

9

Point Four:
Tiferet—Beauty

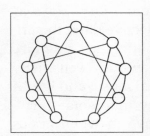 FOURS, WHO ARE CONSIDERED the most self-aware of the Enneagram types, have been labeled **Romantics**. Constantly feeling that something vital is missing from their lives, Fours were wounded in their Essence of **Origin**. They are convinced that somehow they were abandoned from an ideal, original state in which all things were deeply and fully connected. Because they long for what is no longer there, Fours develop a Fixation of **Melancholy**, the sweet sadness of yearning, and the Passion of **Envy**, the jealously that others are being fulfilled while they are not. On the instinctual Subtype level, Fours **Compete** with a rival for a desirable mate as a sign of self-worth in intimate situations. They might feel **Shame** for not meeting group expectations in social settings, and prove **Reckless** in taking risks because "living on the edge"

provides them with the emotional exhilaration they need to preserve an authentic sense of themselves.

The parallel *sefirah* on the *Etz Chayim* is *Tiferet,* the *sefirah* of Beauty. Just as Fours are always perched between the alternating flatness of what is available and the attractiveness of what is distant, *Tiferet* is caught between its neighboring *sefirot* in an ever-shifting, precarious position of balancing the expansive grace of *Chesed* and the limiting judgments of *Din.* Just as human lovers are described as "soul mates," so Kabbalists describe *Tiferet* and *Shechinah* as *du parzufin,* "twin faces" of each other. Because *Shechinah* is now separated from the *Etz Chayim,* because of Adam and Eve's fall, *Tiferet* longs for reunion with its lost love and forms the heart of a configuration of six *sefirot,* which is called *Zeir Anpin,* the Impatient, Yearning One.

PERSONALITY AND ITS LEVELS

Quite unlike any other type, Fours can sense the pulse and emotional tone of a room. For them, mood plays as much a part in making decisions as objective data; the implications and the feeling of a conversation can be more important than the words exchanged. Fours' sensitivity can lead them to creativity in art, drama, music and literature. Fours are energized by life's key moments—birth, marriage, illness, death—and don't cave in when crises occur.

Fours jealously wonder if others are enjoying rewards or emotional satisfaction that are being denied them. Having sensed abandonment early on, Fours focus on feelings of deprivation. Rarely living in the present, which is too mundane and flawed, Fours alternate between yearning for romanticized moments from the past when all seemed right and an inaccessible future when all will be perfect. Fours describe their envy and yearning in the following way:

"It's not so much that someone has what I don't. It's more that they're something that I'm not because I'm deficient."

"Why don't I have what they have? I'm just as special as they are."

"It's not what we've got now which is important. It's what we once had."

"You can get lost in the reverie of your imagination."

Fours' preoccupation with class and beauty is an attempt to embroider the drabness of the present and to boost their own self-image from being an abandoned pariah to being a unique outsider with a distinct flair. Needing to stand apart from the crowd, Fours may flout convention by courting scandal.

Eschewing what can be obtained in favor of what no longer is or what does not even exist, Fours exhibit Melancholy, a regret for what has been lost sweetened by the hope of possible fulfillment in the future. Frequently descending into depression, Fours can react to their sadness by hyperactivity or artistic expression, by wild shifts in mood, or by succumbing to despair and suicidal urges. Because they feel that they have been deserted because of their own unworthiness, Fours can turn abandonment into a self-fulfilling prophecy and sabotage relationships by focusing on others' imperfections.

"Does he really love me? I'm not sure I'm worthy. I feel fear and deep hurt when my partner withdraws. I just want to cry my eyes out."

"I fear that they'll find out that I'm deficient and abandon me. Therefore, I create situations which force them to leave and then say, 'You're the one who is abandoning me.'"

At the level of *Tsadik,* Fours are self-aware, gentle, compassionate and creative. They can share in another's pain and inspire others in their search for authentic individuality. *Benoni,* or moderately developed Fours, are artistic romantics, susceptible to hypersensitivity, melancholy and self-pity. They might see themselves as exempt from the standards that govern others. Harmfully inclined as a *Rashah,* Fours are depressed, alienated, morbid, tormented and self-destructive, and focus on the negative in themselves and others.

THE BIBLICAL HERO: JACOB

Kabbalists portray the third Jewish patriarch, Jacob, as the embodiment of *Tiferet.* Like Fours, Jacob seemed to grasp for what lied beyond his reach. Attempting even before birth to be the elder of a set of twins, he enviously snatched at his brother Esau's heel as they left Rebecca's womb (Genesis 25:26). In his latter years, Jacob was discontent, even melancholy. Having just been reunited in Egypt with his beloved son, Joseph, Jacob still told the Pharaoh, "The years of my sojourn are one hundred and thirty, few and bad, not having yet attained the years of my fathers" (Genesis 47:9).

Not above playing at the edge of scandal, Jacob cheated Esau first of his birthright (Genesis 25:29–34) and then of their father's blessing (Genesis 27). While living in Mesopotamia, Jacob again skirted authority by secretly devising a way to augment his own flocks when he felt cheated by his uncle Laban (Genesis 30:28–43).

Originally described as a mild man (Genesis 25:27), Jacob was later given to great passion. Arriving in Haran as a fugitive from Esau's wrath, he weepingly hugged and kissed his cousin Rachel even before they were properly introduced (Geneses 29:11). In typical tragic-romantic fashion, Jacob longed for Rachel when she was inaccessible. He worked seven years and then another seven years so they could marry (Genesis 29:28–28). Once they were wed, however, he scoffed at her despair over her infertility (Genesis 30:1 & 2). When she died while they were on a journey, Jacob didn't even take a half-day's trip to the family plot in Hebron. Instead, he buried Rachel on the way to Bethlehem (Genesis 35:19). Only long after she died did Jacob again express his yearning for her, giving his sons the impression that only Rachel, rather than Leah or the handmaidens, was his truly beloved wife (Genesis 44:27).

Jacob's great moment of uplift came upon returning from Haran to Canaan. Anxious about confronting his brother Esau, who was accompanied by armed soldiers, Jacob wrestled with the angel of his real fears and emotions, refusing to let go. Although he was wounded in his struggle, he achieved the status of *Israel,* "Champion of God," because he had "striven with God and men and prevailed." In an act of true sensitivity, Jacob made restitution for the hurt he caused by taking Esau's blessing. Offering Esau a large gift of servants and domestic animals, he implored, "Please take my blessing which I have brought for you." When Esau demurred, Jacob beseeched him to accept. Although the less prosperous of the two, Jacob, with rare equanimity, told Esau, "I have everything" (Genesis 33:11).

During his last days, Jacob gave each of his sons a true evaluation of their respective characters. Judah and Joseph were praised; Reuben, Simon and Levi were chastised and told how they should improve. During these final exchanges with his sons, Jacob asked that he not be buried amid the opulence of Egypt, but with his ancestors in Canaan.

SHA'AR/GATEWAY

Hiddur mitzvah is the principle that impels us to go beyond a perfunctory observance of Judaism. Literally, the term means to "adorn the commandments." By using decoration and beautiful ritual objects, we enhance our own aesthetic appreciation of Judaism while demonstrating that God and God's commandments are precious to us.

Given their artistic nature, Fours can find a special path to serving God through *hiddur mitzvah.* Each Friday night, the Sabbath table can be spread with a lovely cloth and adorned with flowers and beautiful place settings, with special chalices for *Kiddush,* the blessing over the wine, and an embroidered cover for the braided loaves of bread, the *challah.* Each festive occasion can be marked as special through its own unique ritual objects; a beautiful *menorah* or candelabrum for Hanukkah; a silver or finely glazed seder plate for Passover; an artistically lettered and decorated *Ketubah,* or marriage contract, for a wedding. These items can be purchased or hand-crafted according to personal taste and inclination. The choice of dress, the physical ambience of the setting and even the melodies used to sing the prayers all help ensure the beauty of our observances.

Memory and yearning play integral roles within Jewish life. *Zachor,* "remember," commands us to recount how God redeemed our Israelite ancestors from Egyptian bondage, to recall martyrs from the past and to remember our own loved ones who have gone before us. Even the High Holy Days are referred to as Days of Remembrance. The mournful strains of the prayer, *Ani Maamin,* tell of how we believe fully in the coming of the Messiah and how we will wait and yearn even though that moment of arrival seems forever delayed.

Jewish tradition can teach Fours and others that memory and yearning should inform and inspire us rather than paralyze and depress us. Examining our own deeds or our own people's history can provide us with springboards to further growth and the faith that renewal can come after tragedy strikes. Anticipating an era of Messianic goodness and peace can encourage us to hasten that era by using each moment to make the world more compassionate and just.

TIKKUN/REPAIR

Given the Fours' penchant for self-absorption, Cordevero counsels in *Tomer Devorah:*

> How should one train himself in the quality of beauty?
> There is no doubt . . . study the Torah.

For Fours who are given to subjective thinking and skirting the rules, studying Torah can move them toward the higher qualities of their Security Point, One, by indicating that there are, indeed, objective standards and values. Caught in their shifting moods and their ambivalent struggle with intimacy, the Torah can help teach Fours that rules of action call us beyond our emotional responses, that there are obligatory ways we are expected to treat others. Rather than yielding to despair, Fours can take heart from the archetype of redemptive love that is displayed through Israel's redemption from Egypt.

Fours who are preoccupied with being classy and desiring to associate with the "right people" can, by studying Torah, be led to see the sanctity in helping the downtrodden. As Cordevero writes in *Tomer Devorah:*

> When man treats the poor with proper consideration beauty will shine. . . . It behooves man to mix freely with all creatures and be considerate of all men. . . . It becomes the wise to deal gently with them . . . never lord it over those designated as "dust of the earth."

If envy caused by attraction to the unavailable is the Fours' Passion, then *Equanimity* in feeling satisfied with one's situation is their Virtue. Humility in seeking a true sense of God through Torah can help achieve such a balance. It can temper the judgmental with a sense of grace and lead us to appreciate the miraculous which can be found in the everyday. Discussions about the Torah undertaken in the name of Heaven can lead to peace and end in love.

When one studies and teaches Torah without desire for self-aggrandizement, *Tikkun* also occurs on the Cosmic level. Engaging in Torah "for the sake of Heaven" helps balance *Chesed* and *Din,* kindness and stricture, while shining *Tiferet,* divine beauty, upon *Yesod* and *Malchut* to our world below.

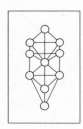

10

Point Five: Din—*Rigor*

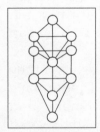 FIVES ARE LIFE'S **OBSERVERS.** EXPE-
riencing the world as a demanding place
with scant rewards, Fives have lost the Holy
Idea of **Omniscience**, of directly connecting
to the world so they can know it as it essen-
tially is. Hence, Fives acquire knowledge and
protect their personal space by minimizing
contact with others and simplifying their own needs. More
comfortable with thinking than with feeling, Fives develop
a mental Fixation of **Stinginess** and an emotional Passion
of **Avarice** as they hoard information, time and privacy
and guard themselves against outside intrusion. On the instinctual Subtype level, Fives can exchange **Confidences**
and bond privately with another in an intimate situation.
In social situations, they create their own niche by offering
their group specialized expertise or archiving the group's
history as if they were guarding a sacred **Totem**. To

preserve themselves, they establish **Castles**, personal safe havens from outer intrusion.

Din, or rigor, is the *sefirah* which corresponds to the Five. If *Gedulah* is expansive grace, then *Din* is stricture and containment. Seen as God's left arm, *Din* cordons off, compartmentalizes and sets boundaries. It provides the exacting judgments that relegate everything to its own proper place.

PERSONALITY AND ITS LEVELS

Fives, who are contemplative people, have a unique ability to grasp ideas, theorize and make abstract or obscure information relevant. Uncomfortable with broad social contacts, Fives prefer solitude. They find it energizing and it gives them the privacy to process their real feelings and revel in personal fantasy. Fives would rather make do with less than become entangled with the emotional demands of others. Having experienced either abandonment by loved ones or a psychologically intrusive family, Fives survive by detaching themselves from their emotions and are perceived as cold, aloof and self-protective. Even when appearing in public, Fives hide behind a pose so they can avoid real involvement.

Fives seem trapped by a sense of emptiness, as if they have a hole inside that can never be filled. Emotionally stingy, they are uncomfortable with the word "share" and are not natural parents. They like predictability so they can preview situations before they occur. They keep friends and interests compartmentalized so emotionally charged experiences don't flow into each other. By mastering grand concepts such as psychology or sociology, and then by locating their own place within these systems, Fives try to understand people and events without having to experience them emotionally.

Faced with either confrontation or intimacy, Fives disengage from their feelings to render themselves emotionally immune or to figure out where they stand. Following this, Fives might make a mental commitment to a personal relationship before committing themselves emotionally to it. Sometimes they find greater ease in intimacy through non-verbal sexual expression. While being able to offer advice, analysis or counsel to those around them, Fives do not easily commiserate about feelings.

One Five described himself this way:

"I'm a learner who is searching for a unifying principle to life."

"I've meditated now for twenty-five years."

"As a technical problem solver I make my living through thinking and I read, study and write for my own satisfaction."

"I feel agitated and anxious in groups. My room is my castle where I can be alone with my computer."

"Sometimes when I write, I get stuck trying to finish it, but for me the process is more important than the completion."

"I know I have a ways to go in developing personal skills and empathy, but I'm idealistic and love to grow."

As a *Tsadik,* Fives can penetrate the profound subtleties of life, seeing patterns that otherwise would go unnoticed. Moderately developed *Benoni* Fives can replace feeling with thinking, demand a great deal of privacy, over analyze details and interpretations while sensing that they must always prepare for the task at hand because they never know enough. As a *Rashah,* Fives can be miserly with money and emotion, reject social contact and commitment, withdraw from reality and view even the ordinary as dangerous.

THE BIBLICAL HERO: ISAAC

The *sefirah* of *Din* is identified with the patriarch Isaac. Seen by his aged parents as the divine fulfillment of their long-awaited dream, Isaac was raised in an emotionally intrusive environment. His parents threw a huge party on the day he was weaned. His mother, Sarah, who was very protective, banished his half-brother Ishmael for mocking Isaac (Genesis 21:9–10). This sense of intrusion must have been multiplied exponentially when Isaac found himself almost slaughtered by Abraham at Mount Moriah, where he was literally bound to the altar of his father's beliefs (Genesis 22). So great was Isaac's detachment from the world after his near-sacrifice that the Bible does not mention that he attended his mother's funeral, nor does it offer any details about the next three years of his life.

Always seeking to avoid the entanglements of confrontation, Isaac moved from Philistia to Rehoboth to Beer Sheba before finally standing up to the aggressiveness of the Philistines and their king, Avimelech. He did not remonstrate his son, Esau, even though he was troubled by Esau's marriage to two pagan women (Genesis 26:13–35). This lack of involvement was never more evident than when he let Rebecca and Jacob claim Esau's blessings through a ruse that led to enmity and the breakup of their family (Genesis 27). Various commentators claim that Isaac's blindness was not only a physical impairment of old age. Figuratively, it was manifest when he let his sons grow up almost on their own (Genesis 25:27).

At his best, Isaac was a contemplative man with great insights. He dug deeply, finding wellsprings and fountains that had gone untapped since the days of his father Abraham (Genesis 24:18). He was given to meditation in the field (Genesis 24:63), and Jewish tradition credits him with composing the afternoon *Minchah* service. When Rebecca faced infertility, Isaac prayed on her behalf so they could have children together. While expressing neither compliments nor yearnings for his wife, as Abraham had for Sarah and later Jacob would have for Rachel, Isaac shared a joyous nonverbal intimacy with Rebecca, often frolicking with her (Genesis 26:8).

Perhaps because he had been separated from his brother, Ishmael, and later faced his own death while being bound on the altar, Isaac developed a deep knowing quality. He recognized the true characters of his twin sons, but knew that life was too short for fighting. Perhaps this is why he was willing to give Esau the blessing usually reserved for the firstborn even though he disapproved of Esau's lifestyle (Genesis 26–34). His hope was that if one son had the material blessing and the other son had the spiritual birthright, they could live together in harmony. When this proved untenable, he gave the special spiritual blessing of Abraham to Jacob, who Isaac felt would cherish it more than would the earthy Esau, before Jacob fled to Haran to escape Esau's wrath.

A beautiful rabbinic homily indicates that at the end of time, the fate of the People of Israel will hang in the balance. Perhaps dismayed by their offspring's misdeeds, Abraham and Jacob will concur with God and let their descendents be condemned for their sins. However, it will be the insights and pleas of the more reserved Isaac which will save his children from damnation. And his many sons and daughters will leave the abyss of judgment, declaring, "Isaac, our true father is you."

SHA'AR/GATEWAY

Study is considered to be among the most important of all Jewish virtues. Indeed, some consider it to be the prime *mitzvah* and many Orthodox Jewish communities are organized with their *Yeshivah* or Talmudic academy as the central communal institution. Statements like *"v'Talmud Torah k'neged kulam"* literally mean that Torah study is equal to all other religious and charitable activity.

For Fives and all others who like to study, Judaism considers education to be a lifelong adventure. If one wishes to investigate grand conceptual systems, there is the world of *Halachah*, Jewish law, which includes texts from the Talmud to contemporary legal responsa and covers every aspect of human existence. One can learn the Bible and its commentaries, the philosophical writings of

Maimonides and other great thinkers or explore the mystical framework of Kabbalah.

Judaism holds that study, *Talmud Torah,* is more than a cognitive activity. It should move Fives and other learners to teach and to act upon what has been learned. Study is also meant to transform the lives of those who learn. This is illustrated by the tale of a student who told the Kotzker Rebbe, a nineteenth-century Hasidic rabbi, that he had been through the whole Talmud ten times. "Very nice," replied the Kotzker, "but how many times has the Talmud been through you?"

TIKKUN/REPAIR

The *sefirah* of *Din* is also known as *Gevurah,* which is "might" or "heroism." This name suggests that Fives, by moving toward the higher qualities of their Security Point Eight, should become more forthright. Rather than remaining reclusive and uninvolved, Fives need to use their knowledge and insight courageously so they can help and lead others. Thus, they can become true heroes, not only by aiding those around them, but by overcoming their own inclinations to withdraw.

In *Tomer Devorah,* Cordevero counsels that we should begin emotional engagement through the love of a spouse. To the detached, he writes

> . . . For your mate's sake arouse your passions gently, providing clothing and suitable dwelling. . . . From this point of view one may arouse passion by the love of a spouse. . . . This should provide the approach to all manner of passion . . . employ them primarily to your partner whom God has determined for you.

Fives often disengage from life for fear of involvement, seeking the privacy of a safe refuge. They hoard their time and ego resources lest intrusions deplete them. The Fives' Virtue is *Non-Attachment,* which differs from detachment. It is being able to experience a full range of feelings without being compulsive about any one emotion, about treasuring what is valuable without being overly possessive.

In moving Fives toward intimacy, Cordevero counsels non-attached engagement that comes not from the passion of sexual arousal "nor desire for gain nor anger nor the pursuit of honor." Rather than retreating to a "castle," the home can be a beautifully adorned place of sharing.

Such non-attached engagement can have redemptive cosmic implications. It balances the stricture of *Din* with the sweetness of kind *Chesed* and keeps the destructive passions in check. The resulting intimacy with one's mate mirrors and hastens the union of *Shechinah* with the rest of *Adam Kadmon* and leads to God's grace flowing to the world.

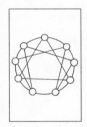

11

Point Six: Netsach—
The Enduring

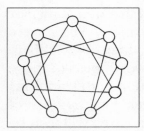

SIXES ARE KNOWN EITHER AS **Loyalists** or **Devil's Advocates**. Seeing the world as a threatening place, Sixes have been wounded in their essential state of **Faith** in themselves and others. Always surveying the environment for signals of danger, Sixes develop a mental fixation of **Cowardice** and an emotional passion for **Doubt and Fear**. Phobic Sixes respond to their fear by flight or by seeking the safety of groups; the Counter-Phobic Six will run headlong into dangerous situations to make what is fearful go away. On an instinctual Subtype level, Sixes will play to their **Strength and Beauty** as ways to counter their fears of intimate situations, ensure the loyalty of their group by adhering with **Duty** to its social rules, and in the area of self-preservation, use personal **Warmth** to disarm the harmful intent of others.

The *sefirah* that correlates to the Six is *Netsach*. This translates as "eternity," or that which endures. Given Sixes' search for safety in tradition and authority, their loyalty to relationships over the long term and their ability to see extended tasks through to the end, *Netsach* is the potency of the Six.

PERSONALITY AND ITS LEVELS

Sixes are the adhesive that holds society together. Motivated by honor and duty, they create and maintain organizations and are concerned with the well-being of the community. Dependable and giving of themselves, Sixes are alert to threats and will defend the weak and the vulnerable. Faithful to their commitments, Sixes are secure in groups with people who have been proven trustworthy.

Point Six occupies the center slot of the Enneagram's head triad. Its Passion, *Fear,* is born not of emotion but by always thinking, "What *if* this or what *if* that?" While Fives deal with fear through detachment and Sevens try to paint a smiling face over it, Sixes assuage their fear by appealing to the practices of tradition, the dictates of a leader or some other outside authority. Because many Sixes were raised in unpredictable environments, they lost faith in their own power to act and in the trustworthiness of those in control. This explains their identification with traditions and power beyond themselves—and their healthy dose of cynicism. While seeking a strong leader, Sixes will also be suspicious of the leader's intentions.

Sixes function well in a defined hierarchy, work against odds without recognition and remain loyal to the group under pressure. However, their tendency to procrastinate can undermine their success because they fear that public prominence will invite hostile attack. Sometimes they place themselves in urgent situations that eliminate the time they need to think before reacting.

Wary of being seduced by praise, they constantly scan the landscape for hostile intentions and might angrily attribute their own unworthy desires to others. At times, they envision the worst without bothering to also envision the best. Sixes are loyal spouses given to long-term marriages, but, they take a long time to trust their mates. They often wonder whether their partners praise them only to seek personal advantage or whether courtship might be a prelude to desertion.

Sixes describe their orientation in this way:

"I used to catastrophize, What if this or what if that? all the time. All I had to do was get on a plane and I'd imagine the worst happening. Once a jet we were on had a problem. My husband handled it wonderfully, but not me."

". . . [Life is full] of treacherous situations. You need to constantly scan the environment to prepare for pitfalls."

"I've been in a relationship for eight years and I still fear, 'Does he really love me? Why doesn't he do this or let me do that?'"

A *Tsadik* or Redeemed Six is warm, hard-working, co-operative and reliable. Devoted to honor and duty, he is loyal to family, friends and co-workers. Able to imagine hidden possibilities, Sixes can be ideal troubleshooters, concerned devil's advocates, champions of the underdog or leaders of the loyal opposition.

Benoni or Moderately developed Sixes can be devoted loyalists who idolize those in power. As team players, they can be fearful of taking responsibility for their own decisions. They can be friendly, sociable and overly anxious all at the same time. A *Rashah* or Unredeemed Six is ripe prey for cults, fascists, revolutionaries or others who claim their simplistic answers will solve complex problems. If Phobic, they act out their insecurities through dependence, self-disparagement and constantly seeking direction from others. If Counter-Phobic, they might project their own sense of inadequacy onto "scapegoats." They can bully the weak, persecute "inferiors" and become hatemongers and criminals.

THE BIBLICAL HERO: MOSES

The Biblical character Kabbalists deemed to be *Netsach* incarnate was Moses. Exhibiting loyalty and an ability to work long and hard, often with little satisfaction, Moses left the palace of Egypt to work as a shepherd in Midian for his father-in-law, Jethro. Later, Moses gave up the security of Midian to return to Egypt and lead a band of less than grateful former slaves through the wilderness for forty years.

From infancy, Moses learned that the world could be a fearful place. To save him from the execution that awaited all Israelite baby boys, his mother sailed him down the Nile in a basket when he was three months old (Exodus 2). We can imagine that young Moses, growing up as the adoptive son of Pharaoh's daughter, was constantly scanning his palace home for signs that his Hebrew background was in danger of being exposed. While his ability to intuit the hidden intentions of others was needed to redeem and lead the Israelites from Pharaoh's bondage, Moses perceived threats at times that weren't there. Once he inaccurately suspected the Israelites of wanting to stone him (Exodus 17:4); he later wrongly accused the tribes of Reuben and Gad of attempting to divert their fellow Israelites from entering Canaan (Numbers 32:1–15).

At different times, Moses displayed qualities of the Counter-Phobic and the Phobic Six. Championing the underdog even early in his career, Moses smote an Egyptian taskmaster who was beating a Hebrew slave. Later, he rushed into danger and single-handedly beat back Midianite shepherds who were abusing Jethro's daughter. Not exempt, however, from procrastinating when exposed to the spotlight or to pressure, Moses marshaled every imaginable argument to forestall accepting God's mission as Israel's redeemer (Exodus 3 & 4:1–17). During the wandering in the wilderness, Moses twice vacillated when his hungry people demanded meat (Numbers 11) and later thirsted for water (Numbers 20).

The greatness of Moses was that, at eighty years of age, his sense of duty and loyalty to his heritage led him to return to the Pharaoh's court so that he could eventually lead an unruly pack of former slaves across a treacherous wilderness. His sense of obligation and obedience made him worthy to become the medium through which God's traditions and imperatives were transmitted to future generations.

SHA'AR/GATEWAY

Sixes seem to have two conflicting tendencies: the need to question and the desire for security. Judaism is a religion that can provide both answers and security.

An old joke maintains that Jews answer questions with other questions. While this is not always the case, our tradition of inquiry goes back to Abraham. It was he who questioned God's motives for destroying Sodom with the words, "Shall the Judge of the whole world not act justly?" (Genesis 18:25). The grand corpus of classical rabbinic law, the Talmud, is arranged as a series of questions and answers which lead to even further debate and response. Each year at our Passover seders, we encourage our children to ask the Four Questions, beginning with "Why is this night different from all other nights?"

Jewish tradition encourages informed inquiry and feels that only at the End of Days, when the prophet Elijah will return to herald the Messiah, will all outstanding issues be resolved.

While questioning is an important Jewish activity, Jews are not left to face life's uncertainties without guidance. Jewish tradition and practice provide us with familiar signposts on the path of life. From welcoming newborns to bidding our deceased farewell, the wisdom of past generations and the support of our communities can help provide Sixes, and all Jews, with a sense of comfort and security, even when life seems chaotic.

Tikkun/Repair

In response to fear, *Courage* is the Virtue of the Six. This courage is not the absence of caution, but the ability to respond to challenges and danger appropriately. Moses exhibited courage by overcoming fears about his age, his speech impediment and whether he was still a wanted man in Egypt. He did all this so that he could free an enslaved people.

Given Sixes' loyalist tendency to idolize the strong leader and desire to impose simple answers on complex matters, Cordevero recommends the following in *Tomer Devorah:*

> . . . Scripture says, "From all my teachers have I received understanding (Psalms 119:99)"; for mastery cannot be achieved when received but from one master. Whoever becomes a disciple of all merits becoming a chariot . . . "the instructed of the Lord" (Isaiah 54:13).

This receptivity to a variety of opinions can help lead Sixes toward the higher qualities of their Security Point, the open, receptive Nine.

To counter Sixes' vulnerability to the appeals of hate groups and to abusing the weak, Cordevero suggests that they dedicate themselves to such worthwhile causes as helping those who study God's ways:

> As a first step assist the students of Torah and assure their support . . . that they may proceed with their studies undisturbed. Never disparage . . . honor them and praise good deeds . . . care for the procurement of

necessary books, for the maintenance of the House of Study . . . [through] support by word of mouth, personal service, financial support and arousing the interest of others.

Not only should Sixes assist those who study Torah but, teaches Cordevero, "When he reads Scripture . . . he has a personal relation to *Netsach*." Such study leads to understanding right action and helps evaluate the worthiness of others' world views. Learning Scripture can also help restore Sixes' lost Essence of Faith because it teaches about God's redemptive love, which gives us a sense of security in this dangerous world.

According to Cordevero, studying Scripture has sublime ramifications. It helps to realign the center pathways of the *Etz Chayim* and brings the divine radiance from *Tiferet* through *Netsach* to the world below.

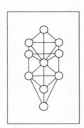

12

Point Seven:
Hod—*Splendor*

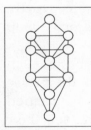 SEVENS, THE MOST UPBEAT OF ALL PER-
sonality types, are known as **Adventurers**
and **Epicures**. Frustrated in the Holy Idea of
Work, which can actualize the full realm of
life's ideals, Sevens flee from pain by using
imagination and seeking pleasure. Rather
than deal with a fearful present, Sevens de-
velop a mental Fixation of **Planning** an endless variety of
exciting future alternatives. To ward off boredom, Sevens'
emotional Passion, **Gluttony**, seeks to feed their vast
hunger for stimulating and enjoyable experiences. On the
Subtype instinctual level, the Sevens' imaginations make
them:

- *Suggestible* to sharing a realm of fascinating
  options with a partner in intimate situations;

- Willing to endure temporary limitations and

Sacrifice to achieve a brighter future in social settings;

- Surround themselves with the security of *Like-Minded Defenders*, who reflect back to the Seven his or her own life view. This ensures a sense of personal well-being.

Inclined to a preoccupation with self, Sevens see the world as a reflection of their own splendor. It is only fitting that the *sefirah* which corresponds to Point Seven is *Hod*, which is the *sefirah* of Splendor.

Personality and Its Levels

Sevens are generally optimistic. Usually blessed with a variety of skills and interests, Sevens can work endlessly and handle several jobs at one time. Easily enthused about new enterprises, Sevens keep group morale up and are innovative because they can intuit connections between seemingly unrelated options. Disliking confrontation and accusations, which might impugn their worth, Sevens quickly replace the negative with more promising possibilities.

In many ways, Sevens and Threes resemble each other. Both are optimistic, competitive and seek the praise of others. Where Threes seek their value in earned achievement and the pursuit of power, Sevens see their worth deriving from their own inherent value and might strive for status as one of a number of interesting things on the agenda. Buoyant and energizing, Sevens constantly anticipate a glorious future and believe in the limitless possibilities of life.

Retaining only wonderful memories of their youth, Sevens mentally recast even painful events. By using their imagination to embroider life, they deny its dark side and block hurtful memory. Possessing a Pan-like, eternal child quality, Sevens have an idealized self-image.

Uncomfortable with recrimination because it implies that they are flawed, Sevens just move on to the next task on their agenda. A packed schedule leaves little time for self-examination.

Sevens love to be admired by interesting people. Using charm as their stock in trade, they'll talk their way out of trouble. They consider no one to be above them and they adopt egalitarian stances to hide their basic anti-authoritarian posture of "you can do it your way as long as you let me do it mine." While enthusiastic about new tasks and able to synthesize novel approaches, Sevens might lose interest in the middle of a project as its scope narrows and becomes "old."

As with work, Sevens can be innovative with relationships. Finding emotionally dependent people difficult to bear, they desire to be close to those who love adventure and a good time. Not only do Sevens want a whole range of activities within their relationships, they also seek the freedom to maintain a wide scope of interest outside the relationship. If a partner nurses a hurt for too long, the Seven will leave in search of more upbeat relationships. One Seven described her approach to life in this manner:

> "I consider myself fun-loving, happy and accomplished. If it wasn't for my positive attitude, I don't think I would have made it through the recent tragedies in my life. My perfect day would have forty-eight hours. The first twenty-four would deal with sales and all the things I want to do professionally. Then I'd need another twenty-four to play tennis and party and be with friends . . . I don't deal well with heavy emotions. I like people like myself: upbeat, successful and interesting."

A *Tsadik* or redeemed Seven is life-affirming, joyful, energetic, resilient in the face of loss, basically optimistic and is willing to sacrifice personal advantage for a better group future. Moderately developed *Benoni* Sevens can be charming and seductive, yet somewhat self-absorbed. They seek wider experiences to keep pain and boredom at bay, are susceptible to addictive tendencies and can be uncomfortable when faced with limits. Harmfully inclined *Rashah* Sevens are superficial and narcissistic, given to depression and rages when denied their desires. They can binge on food, alcohol or substances and might be infantile as they evade responsibility while doing anything for a "pleasure fix."

THE BIBLICAL HERO: AARON

Kabbalists view the High Priest Aaron as the embodiment of *Hod*. Despite the effects of enslavement upon the Hebrews, the Torah doesn't mention that Aaron had bad memories about his youth. Perhaps his buoyancy and sense of specialness came from the fact that the Levites, Aaron's tribe, were spared from slavery so that they could minister spiritually to the other Israelites. This could only have been bolstered by his serving first as Moses' prophet and then as the High Priest.

As a man who moved from one activity to the next, Aaron sought to lighten the spirits of the Hebrew slaves. He went back and forth between the court and the slave camps, helping Moses gain Israel's freedom and then helping him lead the Exodus. As High Priest, he moved in glittering vestments from animal sacrifices to lighting incense to reconciling disputes to annulling misdirected vows. Aaron's flurry of action left him little time for reflection or family.

Like many Sevens, Aaron was unable to see the dark side of life. His optimism and ability to synthesize seemingly irreconcilable options made him legendary as an arbitrator and peacemaker among feuding spouses and friends. However, when a mob pressed him to make a Golden Calf, Aaron accommodated them, not realizing the tragedy and the alienation from God he was unleashing

(Exodus 32). His own activities kept him from seeing the destructive path of his two elder sons, a path that included substance abuse, disobedience to God, insensitivity to women and arrogance toward elders. When his sons died during their day of priestly ordination, Aaron was struck mute (Leviticus 10).

Perhaps Aaron's highest attribution was his life-affirming resilience in the face of this personal horror. After the death of his sons, Nadav and Abihu, Aaron donned special vestments and entered the Holy of Holies to seek atonement for the people Israel on the first Yom Kippur. Rather than seeking infantile escape from his miscalculation regarding the Golden Calf and his bereavement over his sons, Aaron was sensitive to the needs of others and acted as the medium for their reconciliation with God. Because of his enthusiastic, conciliatory optimism, all Israel mourned Aaron's passing, a tribute not even afforded to the stricter Moses.

SHA'AR/GATEWAY

Psalm 100 states, "Serve the Lord with gladness; come before Him with singing." This call to sacred joy is known as *simchah shel mitzvah,* literally the "happiness that attends performing God's will." Sevens and others can discover a true sense of celebration in many aspects of Jewish life.

Shabbat is a time to join in festive meals, to sing and dance and share in the beautiful gift of the Sabbath. The Feast of Booths, Sukkot, is called *Z'man Simchateynu,* "the Season of our Joy." During each of the seven days of Sukkot, we parade through the synagogue with citrons and raised palm branches, *etrog* and *lulav,* and praise God's saving power. At the conclusion of the festival, we rejoice during *Simchat Torah* by reading the end of Deuteronomy and the beginning of Genesis and by dancing fervently through the sanctuary with the Torah scrolls. On Purim, the Feast of Lots, we don masks, rattle noise makers and drink to celebrate Mordechai and Esther's triumph over the anti-Semitic Haman in ancient Persia. Passover, the "Season of our Liberation," is enjoyed with loved ones at the beautiful seder meal, when we eat, drink four cups of wine, recount our ancestors' enslavement and sing of redemption. Births, bar and bat mitzvah and marriage all have their own life-passage celebrations.

Unlike the excesses of drunken revelry, these moments of sacred joy direct us to greater Jewish commitment. On these days, we express our gratitude for the blessings God has showered upon us and rededicate ourselves to doing God's will.

TIKKUN/REPAIR

Always flitting about, Sevens crave action and new experiences to avoid any painful realizations that might come from reflection. Seeking the fresh and the novel, Sevens can lose interest in tasks that have become stale and quickly move on to new adventures.

In *Tomer Devorah,* Cordevero tells how Sevens can achieve their Virtue of *Sobriety.* Sixes were called upon to support worthy institutions, not those that mock others or generate animosity. Sevens should also join in that task as their way to promote perseverance and commitment:

> . . . assure their [the students] support, either by financial contributions or by actual deeds such as supplying them with the necessaries—that is, with food—or satisfying any other of their wants . . . the more one honors the Torah by personal service . . . the more one becomes rooted and fixed.

The Security Point for Sevens is Five, the point of reflection detached from acquisitiveness. To achieve the higher reflective qualities of Fives, Cordevero suggests that Sevens should study *Mishnah,* the primary Talmudic codification of rabbinic law. Because Sevens are prone to excess, this exploration can teach that life's wondrous possibilities are to be sanctified, but not hedonistically devoured. Such study can reveal the gap between self-centered, arbitrary behavior and a way of life which has ongoing sacred obligations and which pulses with a divine rhythm. Perhaps this will help Sevens face the pain and self-questioning that they habitually avoid.

Hod is the *sefirah* envisioned as the left leg of *Adam Kadmon*. By studying *Mishnah*, Sevens help to strengthen *Hod* so that it, together with the right leg, *Netsach*, can properly support the other *sefirot*.

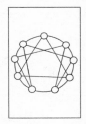

13

Point Eight:
Yesod—Basic Force

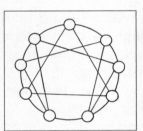 IF ONES ARE GOOD AND OBEDI-ent, then Eights are bossy **Confronters**. They are life's "bad girls and boys." Wounded by a harsh world in which the strong unjustly try to impose their "truth" upon the weak, Eights have lost a sense that a universal **Truth** applies to all individuals. To correct injustice, Eights mentally fixate on **Vengeance**; to hide vulnerability and avoid boredom they develop the passion of **Lust** to acquire power, control and the intensity that comes from excess. On the instinctual Subtype level, Eights first move toward **Possession**, toward controlling the heart and mind of their partners before they are willing to be vulnerable and surrender themselves to those they love. Eights seek **Friendship** with people who will stand up to them and remain steadfast in social relations while seeking to

control their personal environment to achieve **Satisfactory Survival** in matters of personal well-being.

Yesod is the *sefirah* which parallels Point Eight on the Enneagram. Translated as "base" or "foundation," *Yesod* functions as the male reproductive organ of *Adam Kadmon*. In its phallic symbolism, *Yesod* is the channel for the outpouring of masculine generative force. The potency of *Yesod* is also known as *Tsadik,* indicating that, employed righteously, power can be a foundation of existence.

PERSONALITY AND ITS LEVELS

Combative by nature, Eights learn at an early age that the strong are respected and the weak are not. Therefore, they feel secure only when they call the shots and will use whatever leverage they have to win. Able to struggle against great odds, Eights show their love by offering protection to others. Always on the lookout for those who have power and whether they will be fair, Eights can seize control of a situation to avenge injustice.

Because they view the world as hostile, Eights are preoccupied with maintaining control over anything that can influence their lives. They only develop trust when others act without hidden agendas. Confrontational, they intuitively hone in on others' weak spots to see if they'll crumble, stand by their positions or retaliate. They are willing to polarize social situations through controversy to expose others as honest or false, friend or foe. Eights focus on breaking down others' defenses, leaving no room for alternative rationales or self-blame. Fully energized by conflict, Eights would rather fight a worthy opponent than score an easy win. Rather than admit defeat, Eights will bear grudges and plan how they will ultimately triumph when they meet their foe again.

Never cowering no matter what the obstacle, Eights always consider themselves more powerful than their opponents and will fight through injury, blocking out physical and emotional pain. Disdaining those who avoid conflict, Eights see themselves exempt from strictures that bind weaker people. In effect, they want to make rules for others—and then flout those rules themselves. Eights only become hesitant when torn between exposing their own tender feelings and denying them. Their more caring side comes into play when called upon to protect the small or the weak or when they feel they can trust another person enough to risk vulnerability.

Having had their childhood innocence stolen by adversity, Eights instinctively look outward for someone or something to blame. Therefore, they are largely free from self-recrimination and self-reflection. Unembarrassed by their anger, their appetites or their libido, Eights will overindulge in whatever makes them feel good and powerful, including food, sex, drugs, drink or work. Basically loners with low frustration levels, Eights might create conflicts with others just because they're bored by the lack of a real challenge. Eights describe themselves in the following way:

> "I grew up in a hostile environment with lots of random violence. I just had to get tough. Justice seemed tied up with revenge."
>
> "From the outside, my actions might look like vengeance. But inside, its like correcting a wrong, like redressing the balance."
>
> "When I face someone weak or vulnerable, my soft, feminine feelings stir up."
>
> "Too much of a good thing is almost enough."

Tsadik, or Righteous Eights, are assertive, natural leaders whose moral and physical courage move them to fight against overwhelming odds to protect the outcast and the weak. Moderately developed *Benoni* Eights are formidable, explosive and adversarial. They are domineering human bulldozers who show little sensitivity and are contemptuous of those who "can't take it." Harmfully inclined *Rashah* Eights are ruthless, sadistic megalomaniacs who zero in on the weaknesses of others to dominate, humiliate and degrade.

THE BIBLICAL HERO: JOSEPH

Because he shunned Mrs. Potiphar's advances and remained sexually chaste (Genesis 39:7–10), Kabbalists designated Joseph as the ideal biblical incarnation of the *Sefirah Yesod,* pictured as the phallus of *Adam Kadmon.* A closer examination of Joseph's life indicates that, although not physically violent, he did exhibit higher and lower characteristics of the classic Eight.

Experiencing early adversity, Joseph lost his mother at a young age (Genesis 35:16–20). Joseph was the eleventh of twelve sons, and his brothers were a rough lot who attacked the city of *Shechem* to avenge the seduction of their sister Dinah (Genesis 34). They hated Joseph because he was their father's favorite son. Sensing their greatest vulnerability, Joseph told them about two dreams that indicated they would bow down to him (Genesis 37:5–11). They responded by throwing him into a pit and selling him to a caravan of Ishmaelite traders headed for Egypt.

Joseph also exhibited his talent for verbal probing and attack while in Egypt. He used sarcasm when interpreting the dreams of Pharaoh's chief butler and baker with whom he was in jail following the incident with Mrs. Potiphar: "Pharaoh will lift up your head . . . then he will behead you" (Genesis 40:12 & 19). Later, as viceroy of Egypt, Joseph enacted a plan by which surplus food was stored during seven years of plenty and then distributed during the following seven years of famine. When Joseph's brothers came to Egypt from Canaan looking for supplies, they didn't recognize him. He used his powers first to imprison Simon and later to threaten Benjamin to test the brothers: would they now be loyal to each other, or would they abandon another brother as they had abandoned him? When Joseph revealed his true identity to his brothers, he again skillfully inserted his verbal knife. Responding to their concern for the elderly Jacob's life if Benjamin were imprisoned, Joseph asked, "Is my father still alive?" This was a rebuke to them for not showing concern for their father when they had sold Joseph.

No matter what the situation, Joseph seemed to take control of it. Even in his youth, he considered himself more powerful than his brothers. Rising from slave to foreman in Potiphar's home, from convict to trustee in prison and finally from prisoner to viceroy in Pharaoh's court, Joseph always ended up in charge. A decisive leader, he was able to formulate a plan and mobilize all Egypt to overcome a seven-year famine.

In true Eight fashion, Joseph became concerned when he again confronted his brothers. Should he let himself be vulnerable to sympathy toward his family or should he deny his feelings? He then set in motion a whole series of tests to see if his brothers would stand true to each other or crumble. It was only after Judah offered his own freedom as a ransom for the younger Benjamin that Joseph felt he could trust the brothers and open up emotionally to them (Genesis 44 & 45:1–8).

The mature Joseph proved a true champion of the endangered. His method of food distribution during Egypt's lean years provided food for all while thwarting black marketeers. The brash boy who dreamed of growing up to control his siblings finally realized not to use his power for self-aggrandizement, but to help the weak and hungry.

Sha'ar/Gateway

God's call to imitate God's ways extends beyond showing compassion to the needy. It also includes protecting the weak and the downtrodden, causes that naturally appeal to Eights. Psalm 146 proclaims, "The Lord guards the stranger. The Lord upholds the widow and the orphan while uprooting the wicked's way." For these divine goals to be realized, Eights and others must join in the task.

While Judaism forbids taking the law into our own hands, it commands us to intervene when someone's life or safety is being directly threatened. Deuteronomy teaches us not to stand idly by the blood of our brothers and sisters. Therefore, we are charged with raising our voice against oppression and political persecution wherever and to whomever they occur. Many organized groups within the Jewish community dedicate themselves to this task, whether or not the endangered people are Jewish.

Judaism always sanctions legitimate self-defense. However, the example of the Exodus reminds us that God sides with the oppressed, not the oppressors. Eights (and all Jews) should be especially sensitive to the alienated, for we were "strangers in the land of Egypt."

TIKKUN/REPAIR

Given that Eights are prone to excess, sexual license and vulgarity, Cordevero offers the following in *Tomer Devorah*:

> Now how shall one train himself in the quality of Yesod? Man should be careful in his speech so as not to bring him to thoughts that could lead to [licentious] emissions. It is needless to add that one should refrain from coarse speech; one must guard against even clean language which may titillate.

Eights' Security Point is Two, the caregiver. To become more caring and less hostile, Eights should be tender and sexually faithful, sanctifying the exclusivity of his marital relationship.

> The quality of Yesod is the sign of the covenant [alluding to the Covenant of Abraham, Brit, whose sign is the circumcised male organ] . . . Emissions must be

saved for procreation . . . man should not cause himself to become erect except with his wife, in cleanli-
ness when the moment is proper for true coupling.

By giving themselves in sanctity and trust to their
mates, Eights can let show those feelings of vulnerability
and weakness which they have avoided. In such a supportive relationship, they can begin to claim their lost virtue of
Innocence.

Desiring to truly protect rather than control those for
whom they care, Eights, more than others, can take the
primal force, *Yesod,* and use it as a true *Tsadik,* a champion of righteousness. By so doing, they coalesce the divine radiance, the *Shefa,* from all the *sefirot* above and
channel it effectively through *Malchut* to mediate blessings
to our world below.

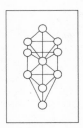

14

Point Nine: Shechinah—
Divine Presence

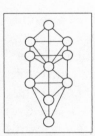 NINES HAVE BEEN LABELED **PEACE-makers, Mediators** or **Accommodators.** Haunted by a world that makes them feel ignored or unimportant, Nines have lost their essential connection to an unconditional **Love** which would provide equality and oneness of all. Their fixation of **Indolence** and passion of **Sloth** develop as they lazily seem to forget their own priorities and seek unity by merging with the needs of others. Instinctually, Nines can become absorbed on all levels with a mate and achieve **Union** in an intimate relationship. For a sense of fellowship, Nines seek **Participation** in social groups and show an **Appetite** for secondary interests and insubstantial diversions to replace real wants and needs in the area of personal well-being.

The *sefirah* that corresponds to Point Nine is *Shechinah,* divine presence or repose. Points Two and Nine both tend to merge with others, being more aware of others' wants than of their own desires. Kabbalists similarly compare *Binah* and *Shechinah,* describing both as the feminine aspects of the sefirotic system. As previously noted, *Binah* is the active female principle that, like the Two, has a controlling aspect and selectively alters its presentation to each of the successive *sefirot* that emerge from it. Like Nines, *Shechinah* is the harmonizing principle, which synthesizes the divine energy channeled to it from the *sefirot* above. Also a mediator, *Shechinah* is the conduit through which divine balance and a sabbathlike peace descend on the world below.

PERSONALITY AND ITS LEVELS

Because they are easygoing and accepting, Nines are generally liked by all. Their non-threatening gentleness and patience gives others a sense of peace and tranquility. Because they are receptive to all points of view, they lack arrogance, can offer direct, simple insights and can be particularly effective in resolving conflict.

Occupying the center position in the Eight-Nine-One Belly triad (See Chapter Three for further details on the Triads), Nines are caught between being "bad children" and "good children," between alienating others and submitting to them. This paralysis is increased because they are also the pivot point between the approval-seeking Three and the anti-authoritarian Six in the Enneagram's self-enclosed core triangle. These conflicting tensions, therefore, make personal choice very difficult for Nines. It becomes easier to stall than to anger others and say "No," to seem to go along rather than to submit while trying to reach one's own decision.

Feeling that they were overlooked as children and not having attracted attention even when they got angry, Nines, in effect, "spaced out." Caught between different factions and unable to effect change, Nines can see the validity of all positions, yet they wonder if it is valid for *them* to take a position at all. Therefore, Nines find it easier to worry about making a decision than to make one. They adopt a variety of strategies that make them appear to have low energy and be slow moving. They can sidetrack themselves by filling their schedules with things of secondary importance, thus delaying important decisions. They can establish rituals and habits with which they conduct their lives, exhibiting just enough energy to go through the motions without truly investing themselves in whatever they are doing. They can occupy their time with energy-draining activities such as watching television, drinking or substance abuse. Even the accumulation of responsibilities can be used to divert Nines from their own real priorities.

In relationships, Nines look to others to help them determine their wants. They seek to know their partners in-depth, and then adopt their partners' values and outlooks as their own. Merging with the other until their own point of view is obscured, Nines might continue relationships out of habit because ending the relationship could make Nines feel as if parts of themselves have been lost. Exerting power through passive aggression, Nines can stubbornly keep others from forcing them into making decisions and then be just as stubborn about holding onto those decisions once they are made. Nines have described their nature in the following way:

> "Being with someone is like being absorbed into their being."
>
> "I forget the source of my own interest and get dragged along on other people's trips."
>
> "Saying what I want if it differs from others makes me feel like I want to die."
>
> "Anger comes as a feeling of stubbornness in the face of demand when someone expects something. Don't expect, please ask."

As a *Tsadik,* righteous Nines are modest, stable and serene. Their openness lets them mediate healing and peace in conflict situations. Moderately developed *Benoni* Nines can be self-effacing, too accommodating, unreflective and passive, ignoring real threats in the hope that problems will disappear if everyone would just agree. Harmfully inclined, *Rashah* Nines can become fatalistic, passive and helpless, waiting for others to save them and then stubbornly resisting their efforts. They can disengage from reality and even fragment into multiple personalities.

THE BIBLICAL HEROINE: RACHEL

Among a variety of possible incarnations (King David being the most outstanding), Kabbalists have identified *Shechinah,* the *sefirah* that corresponds to Point Nine, with the matriarch Rachel. The translation of her name, "Little Lamb," suggests the degree of her passivity.

In the Bible, Rachel always appears in the context of relationship to another: As Laban's daughter and shepherdess; as Jacob's beloved and wife; as Leah's younger sister and rival; as Joseph's mother. She even dies while giving life to another, her younger son, Benjamin. Far more receptive than aggressive, Rachel is usually acted upon. Although she has brothers and an older sister, she is the one who is sent off to tend sheep. She is kissed and embraced by her cousin Jacob, whom she had never met, and quickly becomes the object of his yearning and labors. On her wedding day, her father manipulates her so that Leah can take her place as the bride.

As a Nine, Rachel could be simple and very direct once she had reached a decision. Tormented by her infertility, she demands of Jacob, "Give me children or I shall die." Wanting her sister's aphrodisiac mandrakes, she gains them by trading Jacob's attentions for that night to Leah. In true passive/aggressive fashion, Rachel sits upon her father's idols and stubbornly refuses to budge so that Laban won't find them during his search for them.

If *Binah* is Supernal mother, *Shechinah* is envisioned by the Kabbalists as a bride or sister. She is identified with *K'lal Yisrael* encompassing the disparate spirits of the corporate reality of the Jewish people. When Kabbalists liken the twenty-two pathways of the *Etz Chayim* (see Diagram 1) to a system of rivers, *Shechinah* serves as the sea or pool into which the *sefirotic* tributaries flow. She blends their waters and, in turn, mediates their blessing to the world below.

Seen by the prophet Jeremiah as standing at Ramah and tearfully awaiting her exiled children, Rachel is the healing, unifying matriarch of Israel.

SHA'AR/GATEWAY

There is an adage that states when a Jew says *"I,"* he really says *"we."* Almost every single petitionary prayer and confessional in Judaism is phrased in the first person plural. When Jews celebrate, they thank God, who has "kept *us* in life . . ." When they beat their chests and recite the list of sins on Yom Kippur each says, "For the sin *we* have committed before You . . ."

For Nines and others who treasure group participation, Judaism is a highly communal religion. Not only is this reflected in the phrasing of our liturgy, it speaks to the essence of our prayer quorums or *minyan*. Only when ten or more adult Jews pray together does God's special presence dwell among them. Together, they embody *K'lal Yisrael*, the corporate reality of the whole Jewish people. By joining together, they establish the proper ritual setting where the Torah can be read and where special prayers of sanctifying God, including the Mourner's Kaddish, can be recited. Leviticus teaches that God is sanctified in the midst of the people Israel.

While participating in the community is a prime Jewish value, Judaism reminds Nines and the rest of us of our unique intrinsic value. Each of us is needed to make up the communal whole and no one else can take our place.

Perhaps this is why God created but a single human "in the beginning."

TIKKUN/REPAIR

Of all the instruction given by Cordevero to the various *sefirot* types, his spiritual tasks for Nines initially seem most puzzling. Given the self-denying personality traits of Nines, common wisdom counsels that they pay attention to themselves and their own needs. Yet in *Tomer Devorah,* Cordevero states:

> First and foremost . . . take no pride in possessions . . . think of [yourself] as abandoned . . . [your] heart should be submissive and [your] habits abstemious.

On the surface, this spiritual advice would seem to feed the Nine's personality fixation rather than to prompt growth. However, a closer examination of Cordevero's writing indicates that he is not counseling that we abase ourselves before the needs of others, but instead, he advises humility, especially in prayer and before God. As such, Nines are not less worthy of attention than others, since everyone should stand in awe of the Creator of all who observes each of our deeds.

Cordevero prescribes a novel approach for Nines to confront their avoidance of change and confrontation. Drawing on the imagery of the *Shechinah* exiled from the rest of the *Etz Chayim* after the Fall, Nines should emulate the *Shechinah* and voluntarily leave home on a spiritual quest:

> One should go into voluntary banishment, from place to place, for the sake of the Name of Heaven; and thus he will become a chariot to the exiled *Shechinah,* Just as Rabbi Simeon and his associates used to do in order to engage in the study of Torah.

Cordevero observes that the more exertion one puts into this quest, the greater the benefit. Such effort should lead to fear and reverence of the Almighty, a fear that differs from normal concern for suffering, disaster or punishment. This awe of God should come from recognizing God's greatness, from acting as if all our actions are observed and from worry lest our misdeeds foul the heavens above and debase God's immanent presence, the *Shechinah*.

Cordevero draws on the metaphor of *Shechinah* as an exiled bride who needs to be restored to the blessing of union with the rest of the *Etz Chayim*. By engaging in the Virtuous *Right Action* of Loving-kindness, Justice and Mercy, Nines can effect balance between the Right and Left Pathways of the *Etz Chayim*. Aided by prayer, Torah study and wearing *tefillin* (phylacteries worn daily on head and arm containing four scriptural passages) and *tallit* (a prayer shawl), the proper measure of divine radiance from each pathway can be conveyed to the *Shechinah*. Such a quest for sanctity can, in turn, infuse one's own marital relation with divine emulation and summon the *Shechinah* to be your divine companion when temporarily separated from your spouse.

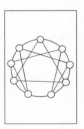

Returning
to God

15

Keter: Divine Crown, Our Transition to the Divine

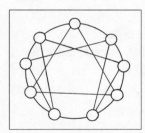 AN INSIGHT COMMON TO THE Kabbalah and the Enneagram is that each of us potentially embodies all the qualities of each personality type in the *sefirot* or the Enneagram. Although each of us is blessed with our own dominant style or particular *sefirah* which is the root of our soul, we can manifest, in some way, all the potentialities of *Adam Kadmon*.

In the concluding section of *Tomer Devorah,* Cordevero indicates that different *sefirot* can be accessed by everyone at different times during the day. He prescribes a variety of spiritual tasks to be performed at certain hours so that each of us can help bring out the higher qualities of the appropriate *sefirah* at its prescribed time.

Night and its tranquil calm is the domain of *Malchut* or *Shechinah,* which is identified with Point Nine. This period has traditionally been equated with death, as if our souls have departed while we sleep. Drawing on scriptural command as well as on rabbinic and mystical practice, Cordevero counsels us to protect ourselves when retiring for the night by accepting the Yoke of God's Kingdom (*Malchut*) by reciting "*Shema Yisrael . . .*" "Hear O Israel, the Lord our God, the Lord is One." We should then awake at midnight, ritually wash our hands, then seek to merge with *Shechinah* through studying Torah. This practice is know as *Tikkun Chatsot,* the Cosmic Repair at Midnight.

At dawn, we should worship in synagogue. Upon reaching the door of the synagogue, recite the verse from Psalms (5:8), "But as for me, in the abundance of Your Loving Kindness I come into Your House; I bow towards Your Holy Palace in awe of You." This alludes to the three Patriarchs: Abraham, who embodies Loving-kindness (*Chesed* or *Gedulah,* Point Three); Isaac, who bows before Judgment (*Din* or *Gevurah,* Point Five); and Jacob, who recognized the awesome beauty of his Angelic Ladder dream at Beth El (*Tiferet,* Point Four). When standing in the synagogue, our intention (*Kavannah*) is to heal any conflict in the congregation, which itself incarnates *Shechinah,* God's indwelling Presence. Just as *Yesod,* Point Eight, acts as a channel that focuses and emits the divine radiance of *Shefa,* so should the worshipper act as a fountain of prayer, emitting praise of God from his mouth.

Since Abraham is credited with originating the morning service, it lets the worshipper identify with Abraham's Three-like quality of *Gedulah* or *Chesed*. During the day, Torah study, which includes Scripture (Point Six, *Netsach*) and the Rabbinic Code, *Mishnah* (Point Seven, *Hod*), helps us embody *Tiferet,* the Four-like Beauty of Jacob. As dusk comes, we recite the *Minchah* afternoon service and identify with its reflective author Isaac, who mirrors *Din,* Point Five.

Even eating can be used to sanctify one's vitalistic, animal nature. If we observe the dietary laws, or *Kashrut,* and also recite the appropriate table blessings, then the nourishment gained from foods can help lift us and our world toward God.

These daily practices help us identify with these *sefirot* and the Prevailing Light, Wisdom (*Chochmah,* Point One) and Understanding (*Binah,* Point Two), which will guide us throughout the day.

Return to Essence

Given the dynamics of our worldly existence, Cordevero, acknowledging that we need the qualities and skills of our personality types, states that ". . . man must perfect himself [in] . . . those qualities [that] flow from the lower Powers . . ." However, there are occasions when the spirit is freed from distraction, such as times of worship and contemplation, Shabbat time and Holy Days. At these rare moments, *Keter,* the highest *sefirah,* can supersede all other qualities and *sefirot.*

Keter, the Divine Crown, is seen by Kabbalists as the point of transition from the Essential, Limitless God, the *Ayn Sof,* to the sefirotic qualities of the divine personality configured as *Etz Chayim* or *Adam Kadmon.* Since both divine power and our world descended from unity to multiplicity through *Keter,* so we, too, can move from our fractured reality to a state of essential union through *Keter.*

Cordevero counsels that such a return to essence simultaneously embodies traits that we can correlate to the Enneagram Virtues. Since *Keter* is envisioned as the crown of *Adam Kadmon's* head, Cordevero relates these Virtues to the head's crown and the features below. First and foremost, the crown is bowed in *Humility,* which manifests patience, the utmost degree of mercy and the *Courage* to do good for others regardless of any obstacle. *Non-attachment* to honor, prestige, material goods or the false superiority of self-worth helps produce humility. *Sobriety* dismisses the options of vain, ugly or judgmental thoughts and dwells upon God's greatness, goodness and how we can steadily do good.

Rather than "harden" one's face against other people and doing irreparable harm through anger, *Innocence* comes through mild action and quelling anger in ourselves and others. *Honesty* refuses to entertain the false and the unworthy, by hearing (and doing) only the good, the helpful, the true. Forgiving transgressions and being patient even with unworthy people reflects *Serenity,* which breathes life, not anger. One's countenance radiates *Equanimity* by receiving with calm pleasantness anything which comes our way. Finally, *Right Action* flows from speaking well and not being diverted by idle or unkind words.

The simultaneous embodiment of all these virtues is subsumed by Cordevero under what he considers to be the major virtue, *Humility*. The inspiration and result of this state is the respectful recognition that the wisdom of God's creation is in each of God's creatures and that "it behooves man to plant the love of Humankind in his heart."

Revelation

After the Sin of the Golden Calf, Moses interceded with God to save the errant Israelites (Exodus 34). At the conclusion of that episode, God revealed to Moses the Thirteen Attributes of Mercy, which Cordevero discusses in detail at the beginning of *Tomer Devorah*. Then, God allowed Moses a fleeting rear glimpse of the divine image as it moved away.

Cordevero, reflecting scripture and Jewish tradition, reminds us that each of us is created in that divine image. However, he warns us that ". . . if man should be like [God] only with respect to his person but not his deeds, he is indeed falsifying the form." Our physical and character structure might mirror that of *Adam Kadmon*. But if we do not seek to actualize the higher qualities of the *sefirot types* through our spiritual tasks, then we can be "a beautiful form but ugly of deed." Thus, Cordevero both begins and ends *Tomer Devorah* with the same spiritual charge:

> It behooves man to aspire to be like unto his Creator, to enter into the mystery of the Supernal Form [*Adam Kadmon*], Both in Image and Likeness. . . . For the importance of the Supernal Image and Likeness is in its *deeds* . . . [through] this all encompassing guidance Man may ever be identified with Holiness and the Divine Presence [*Shechinah*] will never depart from his head.

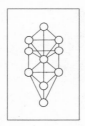

16

A Meditation on the Return to Ayn Sof

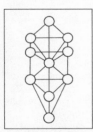 HOW SHALL WE "ENTER INTO THE MYS-tery of the Supernal Form," the path that Cordevero claims will lead us to embody the divine in our lives? Each of us derives the root of our soul from a specific *sefirah,* yet we each personify all the potential of *Adam Kadmon.* How might we identify the passions that obscure these higher traits within us so that we might transcend them and experience, if fleetingly, a sense of union with the divine?

Psalm 62 states, "Indeed, for God let my soul be still." Perhaps it is through quieting our minds and spirits that we reveal the divine within us and beyond us. The following meditation might prove a helpful starting point on your road back to Essence:

Diagram 2 depicts the location of the *sefirot* along *Adam Kadmon.*

DIAGRAM 2

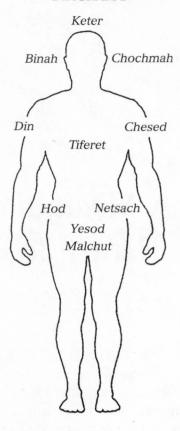

Since we have correlated the Enneagram Personality Type Points to the *sefirot,* we can now locate the points along the body from a Kabbalistic standpoint.

Point One	Perfectionists' *Chochmah*	Right Eye
Point Two	Caregivers' *Binah*	Left Ear
Point Three	Achievers' *Gedulah (Chesed)*	Right Arm
Point Four	Romantics' *Tiferet*	Heart
Point Five	Observers' *Din (Gevurah)*	Left Arm
Point Six	Loyalists' *Netsach*	Right Leg

Point Seven	Adventurers' *Hod*	Left Leg
Point Eight	Confrontationists' *Yesod*	Genitals
Point Nine	Mediators' *Shechinah*	Genitals

During our meditation, we will pause at each of these locations as we envision the *Shefa,* the radiant energy of *Ayn Sof* descending through our bodies. At each spot, we will examine how the passion associated with the corresponding Point manifests itself in our lives.

For example, when we reach our right leg, which is identified with Point Six, or *Netsach,* we will explore the Six's passion, Fear. We will ask ourselves three times, "How are you fearful?" and wait silently for responses from within. It is interesting to note how different personality types refract the passions of others through the lens of their own concerns. In questions about fear, Sixes might respond that they are afraid of physical danger or the harmful intentions of others. Threes, however, might indicate that they, as Achievers, fear failure, while the confrontationist Eights might fear appearing vulnerable and weak. These responses correspond to the Kabbalistic idea that each *sefirah* contains within it the traits of all other *sefirot* moderated by special characteristics of that given *sefirah*.

Just as we will trace the descent of the *Shefa* through our bodies, so we will trace its reascent back to *Ayn Sof*. At each *sefirah* location, we will offer a "healing verse" from Jewish liturgy or scripture which will express the higher qualities of that particular Point. The meditation will conclude by leading us into a sense of union with *Ayn Sof.*

The meditation is divided into seven sections, beginning with Sunday and culminating on Saturday, the Shabbat. Here are some practical suggestions about how to proceed:

- Allow yourself at least thirty minutes of uninterrupted silence for the meditation each day.

Choose a time when you can be relaxed, but alert.

• Find a comfortable place where you will not be disturbed.

• Choose a position, be it seated, kneeling, lotus or prone in which your head, heart and belly, the seats of our Three Centers of Intelligence or levels of soul, can be aligned comfortably and straight.

• Close your eyes or gaze ahead in a soft, unfocused manner.

• Begin with some gentle breathing, exhaling through your mouth twice the volume of air you inhale through your nose.

• If you can, memorize the passions or the healing verses for that day. If not, you might record the guidance for that day on a tape recorder and play it back to help lead your meditation. Speak slowly and allow for several seconds of silence on the tape where pauses are indicated by a series of three periods.

• Keep a journal in which you can reflect on the questions at the end of each day's meditation. Review your journal each day before beginning the next meditation. While no journal questions will be given for Shabbat, the day of rest, you might wish to reflect on that day about your meditative experiences that occurred during the entire preceding week.

Now let us begin.

Sunday
Yom Rishon—The First Day

Imagine *Ayn Sof,* the boundless, seamless divine, hovering over your head as a bright, luminous cloud. . . .

If you can, visualize its color . . . its texture . . . its radiance . . .

Slowly, a beam of light shines forth from the cloud, a beam of *Shefa,* the radiant energy of God. . . . Trace the beam as it enters your body through the crown of your head. . . .

Feel the light illuminate your right eye, which can see the beauty of all things, but too often sees only flaws and imperfections. . . . Ask your eye:

"How are you angry?" . . . Then probe deeper:

"Of what are you angry?" . . .

"Why are you angry?" . . .

Having listened to your inner voice, feel the light brighten your face as it moves to your left ear, which can hear even the unspoken needs of others. More often, though, it listens to flattery and for ways to manipulate others. Ask your ear:

"How are you prideful?" . . .

"Of what are you prideful?" . . .

"Why are you prideful?" . . .

Relax in the silence of your answers and when you are ready, return to yourself.

Journal Questions

- What color and texture did you sense in the cloud?

- Did you experience any sensations when the light entered your body? When it illumined your eye? Your ear? Did you sense any resistance to the light?

- What answers came to mind concerning your anger? Your pride?

Monday
Yom Sheni—The Second Day

Envision the cloud of *Ayn Sof* above you . . . see its light move through your forehead . . . your eye . . . your ear. . . .

Now feel the light of *Shefa* move from your left ear down your neck. . . . Now it moves across your shoulder and illuminates your right arm. . . .

Your right arm can accomplish great things, yet can push others aside as it pursues its goals. Ask your arm:

"How are your deceitful?" . . .

"With what are you deceitful?" . . .

"Why are you deceitful?" . . .

Having heard your answers, sense the radiance from the *Ayn Sof* transverse your shoulder and fill your heart, which knows the depths of emotion, but can be shattered by longing and jealousy. Ask your heart:

"How are you envious?" . . .

"Of what are you envious?" . . .

"Why are you envious?" . . .

Now feel the light move to brighten your left arm, which can categorize and set things in proper order, yet too often hoards your resources and fends off others. Ask your arm:

"How are you stingy?" . . .

"With what are you stingy?" . . .

"Why are you stingy?" . . .

Relax in the silence of your answers and when you are ready, return to yourself.

Journal Questions

- What answers did you receive to the questions concerning your deceit? Your envy? Your stinginess?

- What did you experience in your arms and heart when they were filled with the light? After the light moved on?

Tuesday
Yom Shlishi—The Third Day

Envision the cloud of *Ayn Sof* above you. See the divine light from the cloud move through your head to your eye . . . your ear . . . your arms . . . your heart. . . .

Now feel the *Shefa* move slowly down your spine. . . .

See it illumine your right leg, which can stand firm and true, but instead often runs scared from perceived threats or runs directly into danger to prove that it is not afraid. Ask your leg:

"How are you fearful?" . . .

"Of what are you fearful?" . . .

"Why are you fearful?" . . .

Sense the light move across your hips to your left leg, which can joyously explore all the adventures and experiences of life, but often flees from commitment. Ask your left leg:

"How are you gluttonous?" . . .

"For what are you gluttonous?" . . .

"Why are you gluttonous?" . . .

Now feel the light move to the place in your lower body, where you locate the masculine within you. That locale can be strong and forthright or domineering and excessive. Ask it:

"How are you lustful?" . . .

"Of what are you lustful?" . . .

"Why are you lustful?" . . .

Finally, the light moves to that place where you sense the feminine within you. That locale can detect the good in various opinions from others, but too often is unaware of your own real needs. Ask it:

"How are you unaware?" . . .

"Of what are you unaware?" . . .

"Why are you unaware?" . . .

Journal Questions

- What answers did you receive to the questions about fear? Gluttony? Lust? Being unaware of yourself?

- Where did you locate in your body the generative power of the opposite gender? What did you experience when you questioned that locale?

Wednesday
Yom Revii—The Fourth Day

On Wednesday, time accelerates as we move closer to Shabbat. On this day, the fourth day of Creation, the sun, moon and stars were formed. The very celestial bodies whose movement lets us measure the passage of time. Today, we begin the reascent of the *Shefa* through our bodies back to *Ayn Sof*.

Sense the divine light streaming from *Ayn Sof* above through the crown of your head. . . . Feel it stream from your eye . . . your ear . . . your arms . . . your heart . . . down through your spine . . . to your legs. . . .

Envision, if you can, these beams of light merging

together in your lower abdominal region. Here, the lights blend . . . and rest . . . and harmonize and grow stronger.

Address this place of peace, of harmony, of repose, this place where you locate the feminine in your lower body:

"From repose ascend towards the heavens and sanctify God's name."

Feel the *Shefa* move to the place where you locate the masculine within you. Tell this place of male generative power and strength:

"Act righteously and you support the world."

The radiance now travels to your left leg, that leg which seeks adventure, yet tries to flee responsibility. Tell this leg:

"Keep faith with God's commands and you can explore all God's paths."

Finally, the light rests on your right leg, the leg that can offer loyal support or run in fear. Tell this leg:

"Stand firm and you shall see the salvation of the Lord."

As your lower body is illuminated by the divine radiance, rest in the light. When you are ready, return to yourself.

Journal Questions

- Did you notice any change in feeling as the light began to ascend? What did you experience?

- Did any of your limbs resist the reascent of the light or the "healing verse?" If so, what do you think caused that resistance?

Thursday
Yom Chamishi—The Fifth Day

Feel your lower body glow with the radiance of the divine. . . .

Slowly the *Shefa* moves up your spine and across your left shoulder. It fills your left arm, the arm that can be stingy and keep others at bay. Tell that arm:

"Open your hand and satisfy, willingly, all of life."

The radiance now travels from your arm to fill your heart, which can be divided by longing and envy. Tell your heart:

"Unite our heart that we might love and revere."

Now the brilliance moves to your right arm, the arm that can create illusions or accomplish great things. Tell your arm:

"With your right arm exalt God. Your right arm can perform valiant deeds."

As the divine light illuminates your chest and your arms, relax in the silence. When you are ready, return to yourself.

Journal Questions

- Was the sense of light in your torso and arms today different from the light in your lower body yesterday? If so, how?

- How did your arms and heart respond when addressed?

Friday
Yom Shishi—The Sixth Day

As you anticipate the arrival of Shabbat, sense the light from the *Ayn Sof* in your legs and lower body. Feel it as it moves up your spine . . . filling your left arm . . . your heart . . . your right arm. . . .

The radiance now illuminates your neck and travels to your left ear, which can hear others' unspoken needs, but listens too often to flattery. Tell your ear:

"Hear our voices and act with mercy and compassion towards us."

As the light glows from your face, feel it brighten your right eye, which sees all the possibilities and flaws of the world. Tell that eye:

"Enlighten our eyes, God, with Your divine guidance."

As your head shines with the radiance of the Lord, rest in the silence. When you are ready, return to yourself.

Journal Questions

- What sensations did you experience as the light moved to your head?

- What response did your ears offer to the verse you told it? Your eye?

Saturday
Yom Shabbat—The Holy Shabbat

Envision the radiant, luminous cloud of *Ayn Sof,* the boundless, seamless God, hovering over you on this Shabbat.

The light enters you through your forehead and slowly, the brilliance of God illuminates your right eye.

Sense the light's path as it travels to your left ear . . . down your neck . . . filling your right arm . . . your heart . . . your left arm. . . .

Mark the light's journey as it moves down your spine . . . shining forth from your right leg . . . your left leg. . . .

See the paths of light streaming from each limb and organ all merging together in your lower body. . . .

Now the light begins its ascent. It moves ever more quickly from your hips and legs up your spine . . . to your heart . . . your arms . . . your neck and your ear . . . and your eye. . . .

As the light ascends through your forehead in a single, brilliant beam, you feel your entire self ascend with it as you merge into the boundless, seamless light of Essence, the unity of *Ayn Sof.* . . .

Rest in the brilliance of God and in the Wholeness of Shabbat.

Shabbat Shalom.

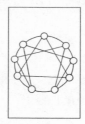

Epilogue
Tseh U'Lemad—
Go Forth And Learn

A rabbinic story tells of a seeker who came to Hillel, the famous first-century sage. He posed the same question that he had asked Hillel's more acerbic colleague, Shammai, who had sent him away in disgust. "Teach me the entire Torah while standing on one foot." Rather than rise to the bait, Hillel instead rose to the challenge. He stated, "Do not do to your fellow what is hateful to you. The rest is commentary. Go forth and learn."

Many students of Judaism quote only the first clause of Hillel's dictum. They note that he has recast the Golden Rule, "Do unto others as you would have them do to you," in the negative, enjoining us from harming others rather than presumptuously assuming that what we like they will too. They claim that Hillel has encapsulated the entire Torah in one phrase. Yet perhaps the most telling part of Hillel's statement is his parting charge: *Go forth and learn*.

If this brief overview of the Enneagram and Kabbalah has piqued your interest the challenge is now to take up the work. For those wishing to read more about the Enneagram, a comprehensive bibliography can be found in Jerome Wagner's *The Enneagram Spectrum of Personality Styles* (Portland, Ore: Metamorphous Press, 1996). The first text written on the Enneagram from a Jewish perspective is Miriam Adahan's *Awareness* (New York: Feldheim, 1994). To ascertain your Enneagram point, a number of questionnaires are available, including P. J. & D. Aspell's *The Enneagram Inventory* (San Antonio: Lifewings, 1991) and Don Richard Riso's *Discovering Your Personality Type* (Boston:

Houghton Mifflin, 1995). A more detailed exploration of your own Type and inner map may be gained by attending sessions and having a personal interview with a teacher trained in the Oral Tradition by Helen Palmer of Berkeley, California. Finally, D. & A. Lewis Lawida's *The Enneagram Workbook* (Scottsdale, AZ: Natron Publishing, 1995) provides a step-by-step guide for self-observation and growth.

A host of books are available concerning Kabbalah. Although very different from each other, my two favorite introductions are David Ariel's *The Mystic Quest* (Northvale, NJ: Jason Aronson, 1988) and Lawrence Kushner's *The Invisible Chariot* (Denver: Alternatives in Religious Education, 1986). The works of Gershom Scholem and Moshe Idel are among the best academic work available on Jewish mysticism. English language texts on Kabbalistic practices include Yitzhak Buxbaum, *Jewish Spiritual Practices* (Northvale, NJ: Jason Aronson, 1990), David Cooper, *Renewing Your Soul* (San Francisco: HarperCollins, 1995), Aryeh Kaplan, *Jewish Meditation* (New York: Schocken Books, 1985), and *Meditation from the Heart of Judaism: Today's Teachers Share Their Practices, Techniques, and Faith* (Woodstock, Vt.: Jewish Lights Publishing, 1997).

One final note: In July 1995, I attended three lectures in Chicago by Hebrew University's Dr. Moshe Idel, the world's foremost scholar in the academic study of Kabbalah. When asked how people should begin their Jewish mystical quest, Idel answered simply, "learn Hebrew."

Far from being curt or dismissive, Idel's advice was challenging and profound. Some seekers today dismiss Judaism as a spiritual path. Perhaps they remember Hebrew School as boring. Or maybe the Judaism to which they were exposed was spiritually unsatisfying. Or maybe Judaism doesn't seem as appealing as paths that are more exotic and to which they are now devoting considerable adult energy, time and inquiry.

An examination of Cordevero's spiritual tasks reveals that they are the stuff of which normative Jewish life is composed: Torah study, worship, dedication to communal institutions, caring family relations and repentance. In addition to prescribing different practices for different *sefirot*, Cordevero reconnected the practices to their pristine Covenantal purpose: purifying the human character and soul; communing with others and with God through Torah, worship and loving deeds; identifying with the Divine and strengthening the power of the Holy Presence in the heavens above and the world below.

None of us should wait until our knowledge of Hebrew, scripture or the classical texts is complete to begin the practices in this book. Waiting will just postpone embracing the richness of a 4,000-year-old tradition which spawned and nourishes the Kabbalah. It will also postpone enjoying the support and celebration that come with communal life. As Hillel told the seeker: Go forth and learn—and act as well.

Endnotes

Section I

1. D. R. Riso with R. Hudson, *Personality Types* (Boston: Houghton Mifflin, Revised 1996), p. 223.
2. This observation is based on two unusual uses of language in Genesis 2:7. The verb used there to describe God's fashioning of Adam is the same term used in Hebrew for character inclination (*Yetser*). Because the first letter of that term is doubled (*vaYYetser*), the sages of Israel claim that each human being has two character inclinations.
3. The phrase used in Exodus 34:29 to describe Moses' face is *karan or panav*. This literally translates as "skin of his face became hornlike." Since the word *karan* also means "ray of light," the text can connote that Moses' face toughened and/or beamed.
4. *Ma' amorot Avot* 5. The expression, "And God said, 'Let there be . . .'" appears ten times in Genesis 1.
5. *Pesikta Rabbati,* Vol. 608 a–b.
6. Babylonian Talmud *Hagigah* 12a: "R. Zutra b. Tibiah said that Rab said: By ten things (or words) was the world created: By wisdom and by understanding, and by reason, and by strength, and by rebuke, and by might, by righteousness and by judgment, by lovingkindness and by compassion." This list does differ from the later Kabbalistic formulation.
7. Post-*Zohar* Kabbalists posited two additional levels of soul, *Chayyah* and *Yechidah,* representing our intuitive cognition and the aspect of our spirits which can merge with God.
8. James Webb, *The Harmonious Circle* (New York: G. P. Putnam's Sons, 1980), p. 510.

9. Ibid., pp. 516–518.

10. K. V. Hurley and T. E. Dobson, *What's My Type* (San Francisco: HarperCollins, 1991), pp. 4, 5.

11. Riso with Hudson, pp. 12, 13.

12. A fascinating panel discussion on how genetic predisposition can affect personality type and attention focusing from early infancy on took place at the Enneagram Association Conference, Loyola University, Chicago, July 12–14, 1996. Of particular interest were studies cited by Russ Hudson and Dr. David Daniels. The idea that, by just being born with an innate temperament, we are already limited in how we apprehend the fullness of reality, bolsters the insight found in some Kabbalistic and Christian texts that becoming physically incarnate in a body is the Fall. Tapes of this session, "Childhood Development," are available from Credence Cassettes, 115 E. Armour Blvd., Kansas City, MO 64111.

13. Given that different persons and different types mentally filter their experiences differently, no one scenario can account for any one type. Extensive background possibilities for each type can be found in Jerome Wagner's *The Enneagram Spectrum of Personality Styles* (Portland, OR: Metamorphous Press, 1996).

14. The self-descriptions of the various personality types in this text are paraphrases of two sources. Some are derived from my own Enneagram typing interviews conducted between October 1996 and July 1997. Others were taken from panel presentations conducted at the First International Enneagram Conference, Stanford University, August 1994. These presentations have been recorded as the "Nine Points of View" video series by the Workshops in the Oral Tradition with Helen Palmer, Berkeley, CA.

15. Riso with Hudson, pp. 17–19.

16. Helen Palmer, *The Enneagram* (San Francisco: HarperCollins, 1991), pp. 49–51.

17. There is a debate among practitioners of the Enneagram. Does movement against the arrow always indicate personal growth and integration associated with the high traits of the Security Point? Does movement with the arrow indicate inevitable degeneration related to the baser traits of the Stress Point? Some practitioners also detect positive qualities that can develop from the challenge of stress and negative aspects that can arise because of past experiences or insecurity in dealing with a good opportunity. Additionally, there is an assertion that under extreme stress a person might "flip" into the lower qualities of his or her security point. According to this scenario, in extremis, our One might become like a Seven who loses all sense of boundaries and commitment.

18. Helen Palmer, "The Vice to Virtue Conversion," Loyola University, Enneagram Association Conference 1996 (Credence Tapes).

19. For the influences of these schools on Kabbalah see Moshe Idel, *Kabbalah: New Perspectives* (New Haven: Yale University Press, 1988), pp. 9, 13, 15. G. G. Scholem, *Kabbalah* (New York: Times Books, 1974), pp. 25, 27, 35, 37, 49.

20. Related to me by Helen Palmer at her professional training seminar August 1995, Menlo Park, CA. It is this reason that my ordering of the *sefirot* along the Enneagram is different from Kathleen Hurley and Theodore Dobson's earlier intuitive placement in *What's My Type?*, pp. 151–152. My ordering also differs from that found in Richard Rohr's *Discovering the Enneagram* (New York: Crossroads, 1992), p. 229. Rohr correlates Point 5 to *Yesod,* the base seminal *sefirah* and Point 8 to *Gevurah,* the power of divine limitation and judgment. Although 5 and 8 are joined by a line, I believe that 5 better corresponds to the constricting, differentiating aspect of *Gevurah/Din* while 8 better parallels the male generative force of *Yesod,*

which is also known as *Tsadik,* mirroring the 8's emphasis on Justice.

Section II

1. The Levels of Development were discovered by Enneagram author Don Richard Riso in 1977. He and his co-author, Russ Hudson, have worked out nine distinct Levels for each type, grouped into healthy, average, and unhealthy ranges as I am discussing them here. For more information on the Levels of Development, see *Personality Types* (rev. ed., 1996).

2. Background information on Cordevero taken from J. Ben-Shlomo's essay in G. G. Scholem, *Kabbalah,* pp. 401–4. Translations of the *Tomer Devorah* used in this text are adapted from Raphael Ben Zion, *An Anthology of Jewish Mysticism* (New York, Judaica Press, 1981).

3. Louis Ginsberg, *Legends of the Jews* (Philadelphia: Jewish Publication Society, 1937), Vol. I, pp. 186–187.

4. Ibid.

5. For the correlation between the points, the Biblical heroes and the *sefirot,* see the preceding chapters. Although Cordevero does not explicitly mention the *sefirot* of *Chochmah, Binah, Netsach* and *Hod,* his use of the terms "Prevailing Light" and "Study of Torah" alludes to them.

Glossary of Terms

Enneagram

Acquired Personality—Our habitual pattern of thoughts, feelings and responses to life's situations, derived from our experience and our innate temperament. The Acquired Personality is necessary to negotiate through life, but can smother our real, essential self.

Arrows—The directional lines which connect the Enneagram Personality Type Points to each other. Movement with the arrow, such as 1—>4, is toward one's Stress Point. Movement against the arrow, such as 8<—2, is toward one's Security Point.

Enneagram—A nine-pointed star-like diagram used to chart the unfolding of the human psyche.

Essence—The original, undivided unity of all being.

Essential Self—The aspect of self when we feel at one with the world, experiencing no conflicts between our thoughts, instincts and emotions.

Fixation—The mental image we form to compensate for the particular aspect of Essence we feel we have lost.

Holy Idea—The aspect of Essence we feel we have lost while responding to the tensions and experiences of life.

Instinctual Subtype—A means of differentiating personalities within the same type based upon our three instincts for survival. Those most concerned with personal well-being are Self-Preservation Subtypes. Those most concerned with intimate relationships, the propagation of the species, are Sexual Subtypes. Those most concerned with issues of group status, one's place in the herd, are Social Subtypes.

Passion—Our chief emotional trait developed to compensate for the aspect of Essence we feel we have lost.

Point—The nine individual numbers on the Enneagram, each representing a different basic personality type. In Enneagram literature, these Points are also referred to as Type or Style.

Security Point—The personality type whose higher traits we emulate when we are feeling comfortable and secure. These are indicated by movement against the arrow within the Enneagram, so that 3<—6 indicates that Six is the Security Point of Three.

Stress Point—The personality type whose lower traits we exhibit when we experience distress. These are indicated by movement with the arrow, so that 2—>8 indicates that Eight is the Stress Point of Two.

Triads—The division of the nine Enneagram types into three groups of three based on their predominant personality faculties. Points Eight, Nine and One are the Instinctual or "Belly Centered" triad, because persons of these types react to experience primarily through bodily instinct. Points Five, Six and Seven are the "Head Centered" triad, because they respond primarily through thinking. Points Two, Three and Four are the "Heart Centered" triad because they respond primarily through emotion.

Kabbalah

Adam Kadmon—The humanlike configuration of the ten traits of God's personality as Primordial Man, based on the idea that humans are shaped in the divine image.

Ayn Sof—The boundless, seamless, unknowable God.

Echad—The One God Who is the undivided, unlimited unity underlying all creation. *Echad* is sometimes used synonymously with *Ayn Sof*.

Etz Chayim—The configuration of the ten traits of God's personality as the Tree of Life.

Four Worlds—The theory that our physical world descended from God through four worlds of increasing physical coarseness. These four worlds are *Olam Ha'atsi-*

lut, the World of Emanation; *Olam HaBeriah,* the World of Creating; *Olam HaYetsiach,* the World of Formation; and *Olam Ha'asiyah,* the archetype of our World of Physical Action.

Netsotsot—Sparks of divine light which were scattered throughout the world during *Shevirat HaKelim.* By performing God's commandments, *mitzvot,* with the proper intention, we can lift these sparks back to their source in the *Etz Chayim* and hasten world redemption.

Ratso Va-Shov—"Egress and Return." The continual movement of the divine radiance along the twenty-two pathways that connect the *sefirot* along the *Etz Chayim.*

Sefirot—The ten manifestations of the divine personality. For a detailed list and description of the *sefirot,* see Chapter Two.

Shefa—The divine radiant energy of *Ayn Sof* which flows along the twenty-two paths to the *sefirot.* The *sefirot,* in turn, mediate the blessings of the *Shefa* to our world below.

Shevirat HaKelim—"The Breaking of the Vessels." During Creation, the seven lower *sefirot* shattered because they could not contain the full radiant energy of the *Shefa.* This shattering caused the *Netsotsot* to scatter and helps account for the initial misalignment of the *Etz Chayim.*

Sitra Achra—"The Other Side." The reality of evil pictured as the shadow, mirror image of the *Etz Chayim.*

Three Levels of Soul—Derived from the three Hebrew words used for spirit. *Nefesh* represents our creature vitality and instinct, *Ruach* is our emotional and social self and *Neshamah* embodies our speculative reason, reflective self-consciousness and high intuition.

Tikkun—The performance of God's commandments with the intent to elevate the *Netsotsot* and help repair the cosmic fissures that occurred during *Shevirat HaKelim.*

Tselem—Envisioned by Kabbalists as an ethereal body, it is likened to a garment of our characteristics and experiences which we weave through our deeds. Similar to the

Acquired Personality, it contains both the light of our higher traits and the *Tsel,* the shadow side of our ignoble traits.

Yetser—"Inclination." According to rabbinic psychology, each individual has two inclinations. The *Yetser HaTov* is our Good Inclination, our altruistic drive. The *Yetser HaRa* is our Harmful Inclination, our drive toward self-aggrandizement at the expense of other people.

Suggested Readings

Enneagram

Adahan, Miriam. *Awareness*. New York: Feldheim, 1994.

Aspell, P.J., & D. Aspell. *The Enneagram Inventory*. San Antonio, Tex.: Life Wings, 1991.

Baron, R., & E. Wagele. *The Enneagram Made Easy*. San Francisco: HarperSanFrancisco, 1994.

Daniels, David. *The Stanford Enneagram Discovery Inventory & Guide*. Palo Alto, Calif.: Stanford University, 1997.

Hurley, Kathy, & Ted Dobson. *What's My Type?* San Francisco: HarperSanFrancisco, 1991.

Lewis Lawida, D., & A. Lewis Lawida. *The Enneagram Workbook*. Scottsdale, Ariz.: Natron Publishing, 1995.

Palmer, Helen. *The Enneagram*. San Francisco: HarperSanFrancisco, 1991.

———. *The Enneagram Advantage*. New York: Harmony, 1998.

———. *The Enneagram in Love and Work*. San Francisco: HarperSanFrancisco, 1995.

———. *The Pocket Enneagram*. San Francisco: HarperSanFrancisco, 1995.

Riso, Don Richard. *Discovering Your Personality Type*. Boston: Houghton Mifflin Co., 1995.

Riso, Don Richard, with Russ Hudson. *Personality Types*. Revised. Boston: Houghton Mifflin Co., 1996.

Rohr, Richard. *Enneagram II*. New York: Crossroads, 1995.

Rohr, Richard, with Andreas Ebert. *Discovering The Enneagram*. New York: Crossroads, 1992.

Wagner, Jerome. *The Enneagram Spectrum of Personality Styles*. Portland, Ore.: Metamorphous Press, 1996.

Kabbalah

Ariel, David. *The Mystic Quest.* Northvale, N.J.: Jason Aronson, 1988.

Buxbaum, Yitzhak. *Jewish Spiritual Practices.* Northvale, N.J.: Jason Aronson, 1990.

Cooper, David. *Renewing Your Soul.* San Francisco: HarperSanFrancisco, 1995.

———. *God is a Verb.* New York: Riverhead, 1997.

Davis, Avram, ed. *Meditation from the Heart of Judaism: Today's Teachers Share Their Practices, Techniques, and Faith.* Woodstock, Vt.: Jewish Lights Publishing, 1997.

Dan, Joseph. *The Ancient Jewish Mysticism.* Tel Aviv: MOD Books (Jewish Lights Publishing), 1993.

Idel, Moshe. *Kabbalah: New Perspectives.* New Haven, Conn.: Yale University, 1988.

Kaplan, Aryeh. *Jewish Meditation.* New York: Schocken, 1985.

Kushner, Lawrence. *The Invisible Chariot.* Denver: Alternatives in Religious Education, 1986.

Matt, Daniel. *The Essential Kabbalah.* San Francisco: HarperSanFrancisco, 1996.

Scholem, Gershom. *Kabbalah.* New York: Times Books, 1974.

———. *Major Trends in Jewish Mysticism.* New York: Schocken, 1961.

About JEWISH LIGHTS Publishing

People of all faiths and backgrounds yearn for books that attract, engage, educate and spiritually inspire.

Our principal goal is to stimulate thought and help all people learn about who the Jewish People are, where they come from, and what the future can be made to hold. While people of our diverse Jewish heritage are the primary audience, our books speak to people in the Christian world as well and will broaden their understanding of Judaism and the roots of their own faith.

We bring to you authors who are at the forefront of spiritual thought and experience. While each has something different to say, they all say it in a voice that you can hear.

Our books are designed to welcome you and then to engage, stimulate and inspire. We judge our success not only by whether or not our books are beautiful and commercially successful, but by whether or not they make a difference in your life.

We at Jewish Lights take great care to produce beautiful books that present meaningful spiritual content in a form that reflects the art of making high quality books. Therefore, we want to acknowledge those who contributed to the production of this book.

PRODUCTION
Maria O'Donnell

EDITORIAL & PROOFREADING
Jennifer Goneau

COVER DESIGN
Bronwen Battaglia

COVER PRINTING
Phoenix Color Corp., Taunton, Massachusetts

PRINTING AND BINDING
Royal Book, Norwich, Connecticut

New from Jewish Lights

"WHO IS A JEW?"
Conversations, Not Conclusions
by *Meryl Hyman*

Who is "Jewish enough" to be considered a Jew? And by whom?

Meryl Hyman courageously takes on this timely and controversial question to give readers the perspective necessary to draw their own conclusions. With the skill of a seasoned journalist, she weaves her own life experiences into this complex and controversial story. Profound personal questions of identity are explored in conversations with Jew and non-Jew in the U.S., Israel and England. *"Who Is a Jew?"* is a book for those who seek to understand the issue, and for those who think they already do.

6" x 9", 272 pp. HC, ISBN 1-879045-76-1 **$23.95**

THE JEWISH GARDENING COOKBOOK
Growing Plants and Cooking for Holidays & Festivals
by *Michael Brown*

THE JEWISH GARDENING COOKBOOK

Growing Plants and Cooking for Holidays & Festivals

Michael Brown

Through gardening and cooking for holiday and festival use, we can recover and discover many exciting aspects of Judaism to nourish both the mind and the spirit. Whether you garden in an herb garden, on a city apartment windowsill or patio, or on an acre, with the fruits and vegetables of your own gardening labors, the traditional repasts of Jewish holidays and celebrations can be understood in many new ways!

Gives easy-to-follow instructions for raising foods that have been harvested since ancient times. Provides carefully selected, tasty and easy-to-prepare recipes using these traditional foodstuffs for holidays, festivals, and life cycle events. Clearly illustrated with more than 30 fine botanical illustrations. For beginner and professional alike.

6" x 9", 208 pp (est). HC, ISBN 1-58023-004-0 **$21.95**

WANDERING STARS
An Anthology of Jewish Fantasy & Science Fiction
Edited by *Jack Dann; with an Introduction by Isaac Asimov*

Jewish science fiction and fantasy? Yes!

Here is the **distinguished list of contributors** to *Wandering Stars*, originally published in 1974 and the only book of its kind, anywhere: Bernard Malamud, Isaac Bashevis Singer, Isaac Asimov, Robert Silverberg, Harlan Ellison, Pamela Sargent, Avram Davidson, Geo. Alec Effinger, Horace L. Gold, Robert Sheckley, William Tenn and Carol Carr. **Pure enjoyment. We laughed out loud reading it. A 25th Anniversary Classic Reprint.**

"It is delightful and deep, hilarious and sad." —*James Morrow, author*, Towing Jehovah

6" x 9", 272 pp. Quality Paperback, ISBN 1-58023-005-9 **$16.95**

THE ENNEAGRAM AND KABBALAH
Reading Your Soul
by *Rabbi Howard A. Addison*

What do the Enneagram and *Kabbalah* have in common? Together, can they provide a powerful tool for self-knowledge, critique, and transformation?

How can we distinguish between acquired personality traits and the essential self hidden underneath?

6" x 9", 160 pp (est.), Quality Paperback Original, ISBN 1-58023-001-6 **$15.95**

Spirituality

•AWARD WINNER•

HOW TO BE A PERFECT STRANGER, In 2 Volumes
A Guide to Etiquette in Other People's Religious Ceremonies
Edited by *Stuart M. Matlins & Arthur J. Magida*

"A book that belongs in every living room, library and office!"

Explains the rituals and celebrations of America's major religions/denominations, helping an interested guest to feel comfortable, participate to the fullest extent possible, and avoid violating anyone's religious principles. Answers practical questions from the perspective of *any* other faith.

VOL. 1: America's Largest Faiths

VOL. 1 COVERS: Assemblies of God • Baptist • Buddhist • Christian Science • Churches of Christ • Disciples of Christ • Episcopalian • Greek Orthodox • Hindu • Islam • Jehovah's Witnesses • Jewish • Lutheran • Methodist • Mormon • Presbyterian • Quaker • Roman Catholic • Seventh-day Adventist • United Church of Christ

6" x 9", 432 pp. Hardcover, ISBN 1-879045-39-7 **$24.95**

VOL. 2: Other Faiths in America

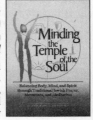

VOL. 2 COVERS: African American Methodist Churches • Baha'i • Christian and Missionary Alliance • Christian Congregation • Church of the Brethren • Church of the Nazarene • Evangelical Free Church of America • International Church of the Foursquare Gospel • International Pentecostal Holiness Church • Mennonite/Amish • Native American • Orthodox Churches • Pentecostal Church of God • Reformed Church of America • Sikh • Unitarian Universalist • Wesleyan

6" x 9", 416 pp. HC, ISBN 1-879045-63-X **$24.95**

GOD & THE BIG BANG
Discovering Harmony Between Science & Spirituality
by *Daniel C. Matt*

Mysticism and science: What do they have in common? How can one enlighten the other? By drawing on modern cosmology and ancient Kabbalah, Matt shows how science and religion can together enrich our spiritual awareness and help us recover a sense of wonder and find our place in the universe.

"This poetic new book...helps us to understand the human meaning of creation."
—*Joel Primack, leading cosmologist, Professor of Physics, University of California, Santa Cruz*

•AWARD WINNER•

6" x 9", 216 pp. Quality Paperback, ISBN 1-879045-89-3 **$16.95** HC, ISBN-48-6 **$21.95**

MINDING THE TEMPLE OF THE SOUL
Balancing Body, Mind, & Spirit through Traditional Jewish Prayer, Movement, & Meditation
by *Tamar Frankiel* and *Judy Greenfeld*

This new spiritual approach to physical health introduces readers to a spiritual tradition that affirms the body and enables them to reconceive their bodies in a more positive light. Relying on Kabbalistic teachings and other Jewish traditions, it shows us how to be more responsible for our own psychological and physical health. Focuses on the discipline of prayer, simple Tai Chi–like exercises and body positions, and guides the reader throughout, step-by-step, with diagrams, sketches and meditations.

7"x 10", 184 pp. Quality Paperback Original, illus., ISBN 1-879045-64-8 **$16.95**

Audiotape of the Blessings, Movements & Meditations (60-min. cassette) **$9.95**
Videotape of the Movements & Meditations (46-min. VHS) **$20.00**

Spirituality

MEDITATION FROM THE HEART OF JUDAISM
Today's Teachers Share Their Practices, Techniques, and Faith
Edited by *Avram Davis*

A "how-to" guide for both beginning and experienced meditators, it will help you start meditating or help you enhance your practice.

Twenty-two masters of meditation explain why and how they meditate. *A detailed compendium of the experts' "Best Practices"* offers practical advice and starting points.

> "A treasury of meditative insights and techniques....Each page is a meditative experience that brings you closer to God."
> —*Rabbi Shoni Labowitz, author of* Miraculous Living: A Guided Journey in Kabbalah through the Ten Gates of the Tree of Life

6" x 9", 256 pp. Hardcover, ISBN 1-879045-77-X **$21.95**

SELF, STRUGGLE & CHANGE
Family Conflict Stories in Genesis and Their Healing Insights for Our Lives
by *Norman J. Cohen*

How do I find greater wholeness in my life and in my family's life?

The people described by the biblical writers of Genesis were in situations and relationships very much like our own. We identify with them. Their stories still speak to us because they are about the same problems we deal with every day. Here a modern master of biblical interpretation brings us greater understanding of the ancient text and of ourselves in this intriguing re-telling of conflict between husband and wife, father and son, brothers, and sisters.

"Delightfully written...rare erudition, sensitivity and insight." —*Elie Wiesel*

6" x 9", 224 pp. Quality Paperback, ISBN 1-879045-66-4 **$16.95**; HC, ISBN-19-2 **$21.95**

ECOLOGY & THE JEWISH SPIRIT
Where Nature & the Sacred Meet
Edited and with Introductions by *Ellen Bernstein*

What is nature's place in our spiritual lives?

A focus on nature is part of the fabric of Jewish thought. Here, experts bring us a richer understanding of the long-neglected themes of nature that are woven through the biblical creation story, ancient texts, traditional law, the holiday cycles, prayer, *mitzvot* (good deeds), and community.

For people of all faiths, all backgrounds, this book helps us to make nature a sacred, spiritual part of our own lives.

"A great resource for anyone seeking to explore the connection between their faith and caring for God's good creation, our environment."
> —*Paul Gorman, Executive Director, National Religious Partnership for the Environment*

6" x 9", 288 pp. HC, ISBN 1-879045-88-5 **$23.95**

ISRAEL—A SPIRITUAL TRAVEL GUIDE
A Companion for the Modern Jewish Pilgrim
by *Rabbi Lawrence A. Hoffman*

Be spiritually prepared for your journey to Israel.

A Jewish spiritual travel guide to Israel, helping today's pilgrim tap into the deep spiritual meaning of the ancient—and modern—sites of the Holy Land. Combines in quick reference format ancient blessings, medieval prayers, biblical and historical references, and modern poetry. The only guidebook that helps readers to prepare spiritually for the occasion. More than a guide book: It is a spiritual map.

"To add spiritual dimension to your journey, pack this extraordinary new guidebook to Israel. I'll be bringing it on my next visit."
> —*Gabe Levenson, travel columnist for* The New York Jewish Week

4 3/4" x 10 1/8", 192 pp. (est.) Quality Paperback Original, ISBN 1-879045-56-7 **$18.95**

Spirituality—The Kushner Series

INVISIBLE LINES OF CONNECTION
Sacred Stories of the Ordinary
by *Lawrence Kushner*

Through his everyday encounters with family, friends, colleagues and strangers, Kushner takes us deeply into our lives, finding flashes of spiritual insight in the process. This is a book where literature meets spirituality, where the sacred meets the ordinary, and, above all, where people of all faiths, all backgrounds can meet one another and themselves.

"Does something both more and different than instruct—it inspirits. Wonderful
•AWARD WINNER•   stories, from the best storyteller I know."
— *David Mamet*

5 1/2" x 8 1/2", 160 pp. Quality Paperback, ISBN 1-879045-98-2 **$15.95** HC, -52-4 **$21.95**

HONEY FROM THE ROCK
An Easy Introduction to Jewish Mysticism
by *Lawrence Kushner*

"Quite simply the easiest introduction to Jewish mysticism you can read."

An introduction to the ten gates of Jewish mysticism and how it applies to daily life.

"Captures the flavor and spark of Jewish mysticism. . . . Read it
and be rewarded." —*Elie Wiesel*

6" x 9", 168 pp. Quality Paperback, ISBN 1-879045-02-8 **$14.95**

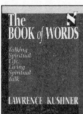

THE BOOK OF WORDS
Talking Spiritual Life, Living Spiritual Talk
by *Lawrence Kushner*

In the incomparable manner of his extraordinary *The Book of Letters,* Kushner now lifts up and shakes the dust off primary religious words we use to describe the spiritual dimension of life. For each word Kushner offers us a startling, moving and insightful explication, and pointed readings from classical Jewish sources that further illuminate the concept. He concludes with a short exercise that helps unite the spirit of the word with our actions in the world.

"This is a powerful and holy book."
—*M. Scott Peck, M.D., author of* The Road Less Traveled *and other books*

"What a delightful wholeness of intellectual vigor and meditative playfulness, and all in a tone of gentleness that speaks to this gentile."
—*Rt. Rev. Krister Stendahl, formerly Dean, Harvard Divinity School/Bishop of Stockholm*

6" x 9", 152 pp. HC, beautiful two-color text, ISBN 1-879045-35-4 **$21.95**

THE BOOK OF LETTERS
A Mystical Hebrew Alphabet
by *Rabbi Lawrence Kushner*

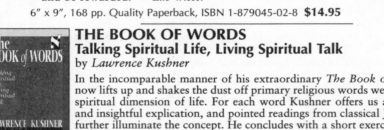

In calligraphy by the author. Folktales about and exploration of the mystical meanings of the Hebrew Alphabet. Open the old prayerbook-like pages of *The Book of Letters* and you will enter a special world of sacred tradition and religious feeling. Rabbi Kushner draws from ancient Judaic sources, weaving talmudic commentary, Hasidic folktales, and kabbalistic mysteries around the letters.

"A book which is in love with Jewish letters."
— *Isaac Bashevis Singer* (ז"ל)

•AWARD WINNER•

• **Popular Hardcover Edition** 6"x 9", 80 pp. HC, two colors, inspiring new Foreword.
ISBN 1-879045-00-1 **$24.95**

• **Deluxe Gift Edition** 9"x 12", 80 pp. HC, four-color text, ornamentation, in a beautiful slipcase.
ISBN 1-879045-01-X **$79.95**

• **Collector's Limited Edition** 9"x 12", 80 pp. HC, gold-embossed pages, hand-assembled slipcase. With silkscreened print. **Limited to 500 signed and numbered copies.** ISBN 1-879045-04-4 **$349.00**

To see a sample page at no obligation, call us

Spirituality

GOD WAS IN THIS PLACE & I, i DID NOT KNOW
Finding Self, Spirituality & Ultimate Meaning
by Lawrence Kushner

Who am I? Who is God? Kushner creates inspiring interpretations of Jacob's dream in Genesis, opening a window into Jewish spirituality for people of all faiths and backgrounds.

In this fascinating blend of scholarship, imagination, psychology and history, seven Jewish spiritual masters ask and answer fundamental questions of human experience.

"Rich and intriguing."
—*M. Scott Peck, M.D., author of* The Road Less Traveled *and other books*

6" x 9", 192 pp. Quality Paperback, ISBN 1-879045-33-8 **$16.95**

THE RIVER OF LIGHT
Spirituality, Judaism, Consciousness
by Lawrence Kushner

A "manual" for all spiritual travelers who would attempt a spiritual journey in our times. Taking us step by step, Kushner allows us to discover the meaning of our own quest: "to allow the river of light—the deepest currents of consciousness—to rise to the surface and animate our lives."

"Philosophy and mystical fantasy....Anybody—Jewish, Christian, or otherwise...will find this book an intriguing experience."
—*Kirkus Reviews*

6" x 9", 180 pp. Quality Paperback, ISBN 1-879045-03-6 **$14.95**

GODWRESTLING—ROUND 2
Ancient Wisdom, Future Paths
by *Arthur Waskow*

This 20th-anniversary sequel to a seminal book of the Jewish renewal movement deals with spirituality in relation to personal growth, marriage, ecology, feminism, politics, and more. Including new chapters on recent issues and concerns, Waskow outlines original ways to merge "religious" life and "personal" life in our society today.

BEST RELIGION BOOK OF THE YEAR

•AWARD WINNER• "A delicious read and a soaring meditation."
—*Rabbi Zalman M. Schachter-Shalomi*

"Vivid as a novel, sharp, eccentric, loud....An important book for anyone who wants to bring Judaism alive."
—*Marge Piercy*

6" x 9", 352 pp. Quality Paperback, ISBN 1-879045-72-9 **$18.95** HC, ISBN-45-1 **$23.95**

BEING GOD'S PARTNER
How to Find the Hidden Link Between Spirituality and Your Work
by *Jeffrey K. Salkin* Introduction by *Norman Lear*

Will challenge people of every denomination to reconcile the cares of work and soul. A groundbreaking book about spirituality and the work world, from a Jewish perspective. Helps the reader find God in the ethical striving and search for meaning in the professions and in business and offers practical suggestions for balancing your professional life and spiritual self.

"This engaging meditation on the spirituality of work is grounded in Judaism but is relevant well beyond the boundaries of that tradition."
—*Booklist (American Library Association)*

6" x 9", 192 pp. Quality Paperback, ISBN 1-879045-65-6 **$16.95** HC, ISBN-37-0 **$19.95**

Spirituality

MY PEOPLE'S PRAYER BOOK
Traditional Prayers, Modern Commentaries
Vol. 1—The Sh'ma and Its Blessings
Edited by *Rabbi Lawrence A. Hoffman*

Provides a diverse and exciting commentary to the traditional liturgy, written by 10 of today's most respected scholars and teachers from all perspectives of the Jewish world.

This groundbreaking first of seven volumes examines the oldest and best-known of Jewish prayers. Often the first prayer memorized by children and the last prayer recited on a deathbed, the *Sh'ma* frames a Jewish life.

"This book engages the mind and heart....It challenges one's assumptions at whatever level of understanding one brings to the text."
—*Jewish Herald-Voice*

7" x 10", 168 pp. HC, ISBN 1-879045-79-6 **$19.95**

FINDING JOY
A Practical Spiritual Guide to Happiness
by *Dannel I. Schwartz* with *Mark Hass*

Searching for happiness in our modern world of stress and struggle is common; *finding* it is more unusual. This guide explores and explains how to find joy through a time-honored, creative—and surprisingly practical—approach based on the teachings of Jewish mysticism and Kabbalah.

"Lovely, simple introduction to Kabbalah....a singular contribution...."
—*American Library Association's* Booklist

•AWARD WINNER•

6" x 9", 192 pp. HC, ISBN 1-879045-53-2 **$19.95**

THE DEATH OF DEATH
Resurrection and Immortality in Jewish Thought
by *Neil Gillman*

Noted theologian Neil Gillman explores the original and compelling argument that Judaism, a religion often thought to pay little attention to the afterlife, not only offers us rich ideas on the subject—but delivers a deathblow to death itself. By exploring Jewish thought about death and the afterlife, this fascinating work presents us with challenging new ideas about our lives.

"Enables us to recover our tradition's understanding of the afterlife and breaks through the silence of modern Jewish thought on immortality.... A work of major •AWARD WINNER• significance."
—*Rabbi Sheldon Zimmerman, President, Hebrew Union College–Jewish Institute of Religion*

6" x 9", 336 pp., HC, ISBN 1-879045-61-3 **$23.95**

THE EMPTY CHAIR: FINDING HOPE & JOY
Timeless Wisdom from a Hasidic Master,
Rebbe Nachman of Breslov
Adapted by Moshe Mykoff and the Breslov Research Institute

A "little treasure" of aphorisms and advice for living joyously and spiritually today, written 200 years ago, but startlingly fresh in meaning and use. Challenges and helps us to move from stress and sadness to hope and joy.

Teacher, guide and spiritual master—Rebbe Nachman provides vital words of inspiration and wisdom for life today for people of any faith, or of no faith.

•AWARD WINNER•

"For anyone of any faith, this is a book of healing and wholeness, of being alive!"
— *Bookviews*

4" x 6", 128 pp., 2-color text, Deluxe Paperback, ISBN 1-879045-67-2 **$9.95**

Theology/Philosophy

•AWARD WINNER•

A LIVING COVENANT
The Innovative Spirit in Traditional Judaism
by *David Hartman*

*WINNER,
National Jewish
Book Award*

The Judaic tradition is often seen as being more concerned with uncritical obedience to law than with individual freedom and responsibility. Hartman challenges this approach by revealing a Judaism grounded in a covenant—a relational framework—informed by the metaphor of marital love rather than that of parent-child dependency.

"Jews and non-Jews, liberals and traditionalists will see classic Judaism anew in these pages."
—*Dr. Eugene B. Borowitz, Hebrew Union College–Jewish Institute of Religion*

6" x 9", 368 pp. Quality Paperback, ISBN 1-58023-011-3 **$18.95**

THE SPIRIT OF RENEWAL
Finding Faith after the Holocaust
by *Edward Feld*

•AWARD WINNER•

Trying to understand the Holocaust and addressing the question of faith after the Holocaust, Rabbi Feld explores three key cycles of destruction and recovery in Jewish history, each of which radically reshaped Jewish understanding of God, people, and the world.

"A profound meditation on Jewish history [and the Holocaust]....Christians, as well as many others, need to share in this story."
—*The Rt. Rev. Frederick H. Borsch, Ph.D., Episcopal Bishop of L.A.*

6" x 9", 224 pp. Quality Paperback, ISBN 1-879045-40-0 **$16.95**

•AWARD WINNER•

SEEKING THE PATH TO LIFE
Theological Meditations On God
and the Nature of People, Love, Life and Death
by *Rabbi Ira F. Stone*

For people who never thought they would read a book of theology—let alone understand it, enjoy it, savor it and have it affect the way they think about their lives. In 45 intense meditations, each a page or two in length, Stone takes us on explorations of the most basic human struggles: Life and death, love and anger, peace and war, covenant and exile.

"A bold book....The reader of any faith will be inspired...."
— *The Rev. Carla V. Berkedal, Episcopal Priest*

6" x 9", 132 pp. Quality Paperback, ISBN 1-879045-47-8 **$14.95** HC, ISBN-17-6 **$19.95**

CLASSICS BY ABRAHAM JOSHUA HESCHEL

The Earth Is the Lord's: The Inner World of the Jew in Eastern Europe
5 1/2" x 8", 112 pp, Quality Paperback, ISBN 1-879045-42-7 **$13.95**

Israel: An Echo of Eternity with new Introduction by Susannah Heschel
5 1/2" x 8", 272 pp, Quality Paperback, ISBN 1-879045-70-2 **$18.95**

A Passion for Truth: Despair and Hope in Hasidism
5 1/2" x 8", 352 pp, Quality Paperback, ISBN 1-879045-41-9 **$18.95**

THEOLOGY & PHILOSOPHY...Other books—Classic Reprints

Aspects of Rabbinic Theology by Solomon Schechter, with a new Introduction by Neil Gillman 6" x 9", 440 pp, Quality Paperback, ISBN 1-879045-24-9 **$18.95**

The Last Trial: On the Legends and Lore of the Command to Abraham to Offer Isaac as a Sacrifice by Shalom Spiegel, with a new Introduction by Judah Goldin
6" x 9", 208 pp, Quality Paperback, ISBN 1-879045-29-X **$17.95**

Judaism and Modern Man: An Interpretation of Jewish Religion by Will Herberg; new Introduction by Neil Gillman 5.5" x 8.5", 336 pp, Quality Paperback, ISBN 1-879045-87-7 **$18.95**

Tormented Master: The Life and Spiritual Quest of Rabbi Nahman of Bratslav by Arthur Green 6" x 9", 408 pp, Quality Paperback, ISBN 1-879045-11-7 **$18.95**

Your Word Is Fire Ed. and trans. with a new Introduction by Arthur Green and Barry W. Holtz 6" x 9", 152 pp, Quality Paperback, ISBN 1-879045-25-7 **$14.95**

Life Cycle

A HEART OF WISDOM
Making the Jewish Journey from Midlife Through the Elder Years
Edited by *Susan Berrin*

We are all growing older. *A Heart of Wisdom* shows us how to understand our own process of aging—and the aging of those we care about—from a Jewish perspective, from midlife through the elder years.

How does Jewish tradition influence our own aging? How does living, thinking and worshipping as a Jew affect us as we age? How can Jewish tradition help us retain our dignity as we age? Offers insights and enlightenment from Jewish tradition.

"A thoughtfully orchestrated collection of pieces that deal candidly and compassionately with a period of growing concern to us all: midlife through old age."
—*Chaim Potok*

6" x 9", 384 pp. HC, ISBN 1-879045-73-7 **$24.95**

•AWARD WINNER•

LIFECYCLES
V. 1: Jewish Women on Life Passages & Personal Milestones
Edited and with Introductions by *Rabbi Debra Orenstein*
V. 2: Jewish Women on Biblical Themes in Contemporary Life
Edited and with Introductions by
Rabbi Debra Orenstein and *Rabbi Jane Rachel Litman*

This unique multivolume collaboration brings together over one hundred women writers, rabbis, and scholars to create the first comprehensive work on Jewish life cycle that fully includes women's perspectives.

"Nothing is missing from this marvelous collection. You will turn to it for rituals and inspiration, prayer and poetry, comfort and community. *Lifecycles* is a gift to the Jewish woman in America."
—*Letty Cottin Pogrebin, author of* Deborah, Golda, and Me: Being Female and Jewish in America

V. 1: 6" x 9", 480 pp. HC, ISBN 1-879045-14-1, **$24.95**; **V. 2:** 6" x 9", 464 pp. HC, ISBN 1-879045-15-X, **$24.95**

LIFE CYCLE— The Art of Jewish Living Series for Holiday Observance
by Dr. Ron Wolfson

Hanukkah—7" x 9", 192 pp. Quality Paperback, ISBN 1-879045-97-4 **$16.95**

The Shabbat Seder—7" x 9", 272 pp. Quality Paperback, ISBN 1-879045-90-7 **$16.95**; Booklet of Blessings **$5.00**; Audiocassette of Blessings **$6.00**; Teacher's Guide **$4.95**

The Passover Seder—7" x 9", 336 pp. Quality Paperback, ISBN 1-879045-93-1 **$16.95**; Passover Workbook, **$6.95**; Audiocassette of Blessings, **$6.00**; Teacher's Guide, **$4.95**

LIFE CYCLE...Other Books

Bar/Bat Mitzvah Basics: A Practical Family Guide to Coming of Age Together
Ed. by Cantor Helen Leneman 6" x 9", 240 pp. Quality Paperback, ISBN 1-879045-54-0 **$16.95**

Embracing the Covenant: Converts to Judaism Talk About Why & How
Ed. and with Intros. by Rabbi Allan L. Berkowitz and Patti Moskovitz
6" x 9", 192 pp. Quality Paperback, ISBN 1-879045-50-8 **$15.95**

The New Jewish Baby Book: Names, Ceremonies, Customs—A Guide for Today's Families by Anita Diamant 6" x 9", 328 pp. Quality Paperback, ISBN 1-879045-28-1 **$16.95**

Putting God on the Guest List, 2nd Ed.: How to Reclaim the Spiritual Meaning of Your Child's Bar or Bat Mitzvah by Rabbi Jeffrey K. Salkin 6" x 9", 224 pp. Quality Paperback, ISBN 1-897045-59-1 **$16.95**; HC, ISBN 1-879045-58-3 **$24.95**

So That Your Values Live On: Ethical Wills & How to Prepare Them
Ed. by Rabbi Jack Riemer & Professor Nathaniel Stampfer
6" x 9", 272 pp. Quality Paperback, ISBN 1-879045-34-6 **$17.95**